MOTIVATING UNDERACHIEVERS

220
Strategies for Success
Revised AND Expanded Edition

By Carolyn Coil

© 2001 Pieces of Learning
CLC0256
ISBN 1-880505-95-9

Printed in the U.S.A.
Graphic Production Stan Balsamo
1990 Market Road
Marion IL 62959
polmarion@midamer.net
www.piecesoflearning.com

First published title "Motivating Underachievers:
172 Strategies for Success" copyright 1992

DEDICATION

To my son Paul

who was my initial motivation for learning about underachievement . . .
and whose successes as an adult and joyful attitude about life delight me and make it all
worthwhile.

Acknowledgments

Thanks to all of my graduate students from the Class of 2000 in DeKalb County, Georgia
who have enriched my life with all their wonderful ideas for successful teaching.

Special thanks to:

Amy Hall for her suggestions of the word wall, a pizza box portfolio and
luggage tag strategies.

Carmen Dillard for introducing me to Webquests and showing me some
outstanding examples.

Marcy Soucy for showing me how she created her own classroom
web site.

Motivating Underachievers
220 Strategies for Success

Table of Contents

Chapter 1

THE UNDERACHIEVER . . .
Who Are We Talking About?

 Brent is a 9th grade student who is failing English. His test scores are high, but he never turns in any of the written compositions which are required weekly. After school, he "hangs out" at a Japanese restaurant where he has learned to speak, write and read Japanese in less than six months. Measured by a standardized intelligence test, his IQ is 140. I met Brent at the Japanese restaurant where he was happily helping out pouring green tea for the customers. He explained that he was failing English because he got an 'F' on his first composition because he didn't follow the teacher's instructions about how it was to be written. From that point on he decided he could get an 'F' if he did nothing at all . . . "and that's what I've done!" he declared with a satisfied smile.

Joanna is twelve years old and in the 6th grade, but most people think she is fourteen or fifteen. She began maturing physically in the 5th grade, and her As and Bs slipped to Cs and Ds. She's interested in going to the skating rink on week-ends and in meeting boys. She says she doesn't want the boys to know she is smart, because if they did, they wouldn't think she was "cool."

Leo is having lots of problems at home. His parents went through a divorce two years ago and his dad often fails to send the child support check. It seems to Leo that his mother is always unhappy. She has a job, but it isn't enough to make ends meet. Leo is in 7th grade and finds school hard. His teachers think he is a behavior problem. He knows he should study, but he really doesn't feel like it in school and he doesn't feel like it when he gets home from school either. He used to think he was smart enough to get a college scholarship someday, but he just doesn't care about that — or about much of anything — anymore.

 Paul loves school, though he cares little if at all about schoolwork. He considers school a wonderful place to find a willing and attentive audience for his latest antics. He drives his teachers crazy, but he makes his classmates laugh! Paul is never absent, and his classmates can hardly wait to see what he will do next. Things that are important to teachers and administrators such as test scores, report card grades, homework, and study skills are quite meaningless to Paul. If an adult talks to him about improving his achievement, he asks them to chill out and not get so stressed about things!

All four of the students described are underachievers. They are representative of thousands of students who are not achieving academically or socially in school, yet have the potential to do so. Each represents a certain prototype of an underachiever.

* Brent is the type of student who marches to the beat of his own drummer. He doesn't think rules or instructions are meant for him, so he typically ignores them. If there is a consequence for doing this, a student like Brent will blame the teacher or the system but will not take the responsibility for his own actions. Many of these underachievers learn outside of the classroom but rebel when they are told they must follow classroom rules or school regulations.

* Joanna represents adolescent females who deliberately decide to underachieve and pretend they aren't very smart. These girls typically develop academic holes in one or two subjects. They miss instruction in significant academic concepts or get behind in their assignments. Before long, their pretense has become a self-fulfilling prophesy.

* Leo is the saddest of my prototypes. He exemplifies students who have problems and concerns outside of school that almost always impact what is going on in school as well. These students often have little or no support at home. They come from unstable families or families where there are so many problems that school is the last thing on their minds.

* Paul typifies the "class clown." Usually a happy-go-lucky student, the class clown enjoys school and is popular with his or her classmates. Underachievement results because so little effort is put into formal learning and work. Sometimes the class clown is also the class manipulator, seeing how much he can get away with or how much work he can avoid.

UNDERACHIEVEMENT
What is it?

Underachievement is one of those popular "catchall" terms that means something different to nearly everyone who hears it. In one sense, we are all underachievers. Studies have been done which show that all humans use only a small percentage of their total brain capacity. Additionally, most of us could pinpoint projects or activities, tests or papers where we could have put forth more effort than we actually did. Almost everyone can recall something in which they could have done a better job. However, the underachieving students we are focusing on in this book are more than this. These students have a significant gap between their ability and what they produce and achieve in the classroom.

Various researchers have quantified underachievement:

- Underachievement can be defined as a discrepancy between the child's school performance and some index of his or her actual ability. Ability may be measured by test scores or even by observing the child at home or at school. (Rimm)

- Underachieving students have a gap between achievement test scores and intelligence test scores or between academic grades and intelligence test scores. (Gallagher)

- A child achieving significantly below the level statistically predicted by his/her IQ. (Newman)

- One whose achievement score is lower than his/her ability score. (Kowitz)

- When a child with a high IQ has low grades in school (Ziv)

To my mind, underachievers are students who, in a significant way, are not working up to their potential. These students often see "YOU CAN DO BETTER" written boldly in red on homework and test papers, and receive this message in many other ways, both verbally and nonverbally. However, for a variety of reasons they continue to do much less than they are capable of doing.

Underachievement can be considered an "umbrella" term. I am often asked about the relationship between underachievement and various learning difficulties such as learning disabilities, behavioral disorders, ADD and ADHD. These are *types* of underachievement. However, underachievement does not only indicate specific disorders. Instead, it is a generic term and encompasses much more than that.

Underachievement is usually <u>degenerative</u>. Signs begin in the early grades and the effects are cumulative as the child grows older. While signs of underachievement often begin as early as the third or fourth grade, middle school or junior high usually marks the highest point of consistent under-achievement.

A graph of a typical underachiever's school success may appear as:

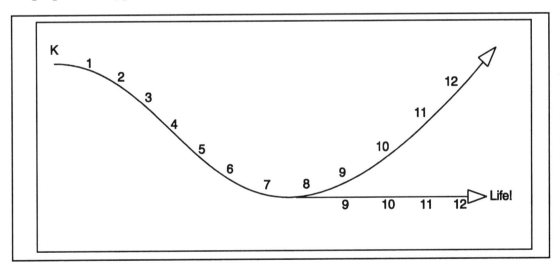

Interestingly, some underachievers seem to reverse their underachievement during high school. Maybe they see the possibility of graduation and "real life." Perhaps they simply mature a bit. But for many others, underachievement isn't reversed. It continues well into adulthood and in fact, may continue all through life. Thus, it is essential that we work with students to help them reverse this underachieving pattern as early in their school life as possible.

CHARACTERISTICS OF UNDERACHIEVERS

What types of kids are underachievers? How do they differ from achieving students both in and out of school? The answers to these questions may help us understand ways we can best work with and help these students.

In studies comparing underachievers and high achievers, a significant difference in self concept, school attitudes, and out of school pursuits is shown between the two groups. Behaviorally, underachievers are often described as "immature" or "behavior problems." Most lack motivation for schoolwork and say that they are bored with school. They have low self esteem and a fear of failure. Underachieving students usually lack basic study skills.

The School

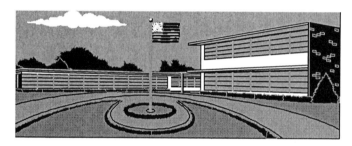 Reasons for underachievement may come from the school. Some teachers have impossible standards while others may have low expectations for their students. Either way, underachievement can result. Other teachers are too strict or repressive and lack patience with students who ask difficult questions, who do not conform, are who are divergent rather than convergent thinkers, etc. This type of classroom climate eventually turns students off to school.

Many times, the make-up of the school system itself contributes to underachievement. The conforming nature of the school setting, inappropriate or dull curricula, days and weeks spent on drill and practice activities for standardized tests, and inflexibility in scheduling, types of activities, or curricular content can lead to underachievement in many students.

The vast majority of underachieving elementary school students are boys. This is due, in part, to the traditional structure of the school itself with its emphasis on straight rows of desks, quiet learning, and compliant behavior. Such a school setting is usually more suitable for girls than boys.

Less noticed, perhaps, are the underachieving girls of middle school and high school age. Girls who have done well in elementary school suddenly develop an interest in boys and decide it isn't "cool" to be so smart. Many prefer not to demonstrate their intelligence, feeling that if they do, the boys will not like them as much. A column for teens in a popular weekly magazine posed the question, "Have you ever pretended to be something you're not?" Although this was not a question about school, girls' replies to it illustrate well the mindset which often leads to underachievement in adolescent females:

Sometimes I act like I'm not as intelligent as I really am. I feel that if guys knew that I have a 4.0 average, they would be intimidated. In fact, I've found that to be true. (Age 14)

In our school it's "cool" to fail and be stupid. So sometimes I've pretended that I'm not that smart. If I do well, I deny it by saying "I didn't study." (Age 16)

I have about a 3.8 average, but I act so dumb sometimes that people who don't know me well think I'm really stupid, especially since I'm a girl. I have so much ambivalence about it. (Age 17)

The Home

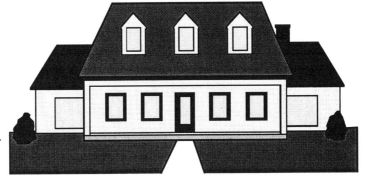

Underachievers often come from homes where there is considerable instability within the family unit. Since so many families are in turmoil, under stress or over-committed, it is easy to see why underachievement is on the rise. When families have other worries to deal with, such as marital discord, job pressures, financial concerns, a lack of emotional support, no leisure or family time, and isolation from extended family, education becomes less of a priority.

In some families, just surviving from day to day is the focus of life. In others, the complexity of modern life with all its busyness has taken its toll. In both situations, a child's achievement in school does not really seem important. Still other parents demand high grades of their children without any concern as to whether they are actually learning anything. To these parents, the report card is the important concern, not the learning that has or has not taken place!

Well-meaning parents who place a high priority on educational achievement sometimes put too much pressure on their children to achieve in school. "Counter identification" may result, where a parent overly identifies with the successes and failures of a child. In this situation, the parent may almost be living his or her life through the child, and the child may feel he or she could never live up to parental expectations. Many times, one child in a family will become a high achiever while the other will rebel against the pressure to succeed.

For parents, being an encourager of educational achievement without exerting undo pressure requires striking a delicate balance. There is no magic "balancing formula," thus each parent will have to decide where that point of balance is with each child.

What can we do with underachievers?

As I have worked with teachers and parents during the past several years, I have heard this question over and over again. There is no one answer, but multiple answers and strategies. Self esteem, study skills, motivation, parent/teacher collaboration . . . all play a role in solving the puzzle of underachievement.

The purpose of this book is to share some answers by presenting a multitude of strategies that work with underachievers. Not all strategies will work with all students; the intent is that the reader pick the ones that look as if they will be workable with an individual student in a given situation and try them.

The strategies in this book (220 in all) are numbered for easy reference. Pick and choose among them. I hope they will be helpful to you and your students.

- Carolyn Coil

Chapter 2

BUILDING SELF ESTEEM

A healthy self-image is one of the greatest assets we can possess.

THOUGHTS ON CHANGING SELF CONCEPT

> *"This kid is just not motivated! He doesn't seem to care about anything we're doing in class. He rarely turns in an assignment, and when he does, I have the feeling he could have done the work so much better. He will get a D in my class this grading period. I've been on him since September about his work and have even shown his work to the class as an example of what not to do. I guess he's just impossible. He should try harder."*

The student described above is typical of many underachievers. He seems to be unmotivated, but this lack of motivation is tied directly to his low self concept. Some teachers feel that nothing can be done with this type of student. I believe, however, that it is possible to change self concept, and further, that the change can be either in a positive or negative direction. The change results, for the most part, from the messages the child receives about himself or herself from others. At school, these messages come from teachers and peers. What other people say and how they act definitely impacts on children's central beliefs about themselves.

I wonder what the student described above will remember about his school years and the messages about himself he received from teachers. In workshops, I often ask participants to recall one instance from their childhood where they felt "put down" or embarrassed by a remark from a teacher. I am constantly amazed that memories from twenty, thirty, forty and even fifty years in the past are still vividly there. From one teacher:

The art teacher came to our room once a week. My first rec-ollection of art was a picture we were to draw of a bank, water, a tree, clouds and the sun. The teacher wanted our pic-ture to look "just like" hers. I was overjoyed at the prospect of using a paintbrush and paints! But, alas, the art teacher hated my painting. She held it up to the entire class as an example of how not to paint. It was not until I took art in college that I was able to dispel the horror I felt toward "art projects."

A memory from another teacher:

When I was in 4th grade, on the way to PE class my teacher informed me that I asked too many questions in class. My questions always pertained to the subject matter we were discussing. However, she felt they were in excess. She then proceeded to tell me that she would no longer answer my questions. This made such an impact on me that it has only been in the last few years that I've overcome the feeling that I should not ask questions. I always encourage my students to stop me at anytime to ask questions. I think everyone benefits from this and certainly do not think children should be discouraged from speaking up.

Self esteem comes from people's **perceptions** about what other people think of them. These perceptions are the result of information that comes from outside sources such as parents and teachers. Positive and negative messages both affect self esteem.

Self concept is formed from the self esteem each person has. In the two cases cited above, self concept was changed and self esteem was lowered by the offhand remarks of a teacher. The teachers making these remarks probably thought very little about what they had said. Yet their words still echo in the minds of these adult women forty or fifty years after they were uttered. As teachers, we don't realize the impact our words can have! These examples illustrate the effect of negative feedback and how it can hurt self esteem.

Positive feedback can be equally as powerful in building self esteem. Many teachers feel they cannot make a difference in the lives of the students they teach. The facts tell a different story. Teachers do make an impact on the self esteem of their students. The strategies discussed in the following pages will give you some ideas for building up your students and impacting them in a positive way. Helping students to build a positive self concept is one of the most effective ways to turn underachievers into achievers.

> This chapter is divided into two main sections:
> - Positive Communication and Legitimate Praise
> - Helping Students in Self Discovery
>
> Each section focuses, in a little different way, on successful strategies for building positive self concept in underachieving students.

POSITIVE COMMUNICATION AND LEGITIMATE PRAISE:
THE BUILDING BLOCKS OF SELF ESTEEM

Successful Strategies . . .

Avoid Put Downs

1. Make sure your words or actions cannot be interpreted as rejection.

How easy it is for a teacher to make an offhand remark that can be taken as rejection by an overly sensitive child! The difficulty lies in the fact that this is a judgment call. The same remark may be interpreted as rejection by one child yet may be needed verbal guidance for another. The key is **knowing your students** well enough to make these judgment calls.

2. Be careful not to use sarcasm or say something which could be interpreted as a "put down."

Sarcastic remarks are truly tempting! With upper elementary and middle school students in particular, such remarks often bring laughter from the class, but at the expense of the student being laughed at. Avoid the temptation to use sarcastic verbal put-downs. The cost in a student's self esteem is just too great.

3. Correct the child privately when verbal discipline is necessary.

A well-disciplined class is a necessity in order for teaching and learning to occur. Enforcement of class rules and establishing behavioral norms are important parts of achieving this goal. On an individual level, however, behavioral management is more effective when it is done privately. The child involved does not become "the bad kid" in the eyes of his/her classmates and does not have to live up to such an image as the days and weeks of school go by. Underachievers often achieve in living up to the "bad kid" role they find themselves in. One way of avoiding underachievement is not reinforcing the "bad kid" image.

4. Encourage parents and other teachers to see the underachieving child in a positive way.

Become an advocate for one of your underachievers! Underachieving students are often the topic of complaints in the faculty lounge, with each teacher chiming in with a different "horror story." Talking with parents often yields the same result. While others are addressing the child's weaknesses, identify a strength and comment on its positive attributes.

Build on Strengths

5. Notice and comment to the child on his/her unique qualities, strengths, and capabilities.

All children have strengths, but underachievers are usually unaware of what their own strengths are. A verbal, positive acknowledgment of a strength can have a far reaching impact. Any desirable trait or behavior - thoughtfulness, creativity, interests, effort, or a job well done can and should be acknowledged.

6. Work with the student's strengths thereby giving him/her the opportunity to feel successful.

A step beyond acknowledgment, strengths must be built upon and nurtured. Nothing motivates more than the experience of success. Many underachievers feel they are failures, for they have so much experience in this realm. Building on a strength to bring an initial successful experience will usually be repeated with other successes.

7. Identify strengths and weaknesses using the assessment instruments on the next two pages.

Many times parents, teachers, and guidance counselors who work closely with underachievers have difficulty identifying specific strengths which the child may have. These assessment instruments provide a means of getting an overview of specific strengths and weaknesses in both the affective and academic areas. You may be surprised at some of the strengths your underachiever already possesses! Use these instruments to help you in building on strengths and remediating weaknesses. For many students, seeing their strengths and weaknesses on paper in an easy-to-read format is the first step in setting some goals for improvement. When using these assessment tools, emphasize strengths while attempting to work on one or two weaknesses at a time. Students with an abundance of weaknesses will be overwhelmed if they are asked to work on too many at one time.

8. Have students identify their own strengths and weaknesses.

Adults are not the only ones who struggle to identify the strengths of underachievers. The students themselves need to learn how to identify their own strengths as well as their weaknesses. One way to do this is to provide them with a checklist where they identify their strengths first and then identify a limited number of weaknesses. This checklist can be used as a springboard for a small group or classroom activity celebrating student strengths. Sample checklists can be found in Becoming an Achiever by Carolyn Coil, Pieces of Learning, publisher.

AFFECTIVE CHARACTERISTICS OF STUDENTS WHO ARE BECOMING ACHIEVERS . . .

Are your underachievers showing strength in any of these areas?

Student's Name _____

> For a quick overview of an individual child,
> mark **S** to indicate **Strength**:
> mark **W** to indicate **Weakness**
> in the items listed below.

___1. Has a high, yet realistic, self concept.

___2. Communicates problems and concerns with teachers and works to solve them.

___3. Is a risk-taker.

___4. Is willing to work to change areas of dissatisfaction.

___5. Listens to those in authority over him/her.

___6. Takes responsibility for problems and does not put all of the blame on others.

___7. Functions reasonably well in a group which is working on something constructive.

___8. Has a close friend or friends who share similar interests which are socially acceptable.

___9. Is flexible and can see more than one possible solution when solving a problem.

___10. Has an area of intense interest.

___11. Practices self-discipline and self-control.

___12. Uses influence over others in a positive way.

___13. Has a positive attitude toward school.

___14. Recognizes his/her contribution to negative situations or behavior problems as they occur.

___15. Chooses peers who are achievers and have positive attitudes about school.

___16. Attempts to display appropriate behavior.

(Add your own)

___17.

___18.

Reproducible page for teacher use.

ACADEMIC CHARACTERISTICS OF STUDENTS WHO ARE BECOMING ACHIEVERS . . .

Are your underachievers showing strength in any of these areas?

Student's Name _____

> For a quick overview of an individual child,
> mark **S** to indicate **Strength**:
> mark **W** to indicate **Weakness**
> in the items listed below.

___1. Feels that at least one subject/topic/class in school is interesting and worthwhile.

___2. Exhibits organizational and time management skills.

___3. Is able to comprehend reading assignments in the content areas.

___4. Finds it easy to memorize unfamiliar information.

___5. Shows pride in the quality of his/her schoolwork.

___6. Is persistent in working on subjects that don't come easily.

___7. Has a good attention span and is able to concentrate on assigned tasks.

___8. Is punctual and has good attendance.

___9. Is open to obtaining help and remediation of academic weaknesses.

___10. Works to improve when grades or test scores are low.

___11. Sets short term and long term goals.

___12. In some subjects is willing to do more than just "get by."

___13. Shows creativity at home or at school.

___14. Sees the relationship between achievement in school and future success.

(Add your own)

___15.

___16.

Reproducible page for teacher use.

Give Positive Feedback

9. Give individualized feedback, support and encouragement.

Teachers work hard to individualize instruction and differentiate curriculum, even when faced with large class sizes. In the same way, it's important to individualize feedback beyond marking correct and incorrect answers on papers. The time spent doing this is well worth it. Some learners will appreciate written comments while other learners will ignore the written feedback but will pay close attention to what you say. Learn which type of feedback works best with each of your students.

10. Give specific, sincere, praise often, describing what you see and how you feel about it. This tells a child that you have really taken the time to notice what he's done.

A number of research studies indicate that the more specific the praise, the more effective it is. Underachieving students don't hear specific praise very often, and they interpret generalized praise as insincere. Target areas in which you can give specific, sincere praise along with reasons for that praise to your underachievers.

11. Let the child know what you like and appreciate about him or her.

All children have likable qualities. An underachiever hears so much about his/her negative qualities that the likable qualities are lost in the shuffle. Find something that you like about your underachiever. This quality does not need to be related to academics. Give compliments. Recognition and appreciation are the important things.

12. Let your children know that you are glad to be a teacher, and, more specifically, that you are glad to be their teacher.

Teacher morale is at a low point in many school districts. Faced with budget cuts, stringent accountability measures, bad press and a lack of respect, many teachers are discouraged. Unfortunately, students tune into this discouragement, and it spills over onto their feelings about school. Counteract this by enjoying your students and your classes, and letting your students know that you feel it's great to be a teacher.

13. Use expressions of courtesy in interactions with students.

Treating others with courtesy seems to be a lost art. Even the word 'courtesy' has an old-fashioned ring about it! Webster's dictionary defines it as "gracious politeness." Yet in an age of extreme rudeness and disrespect, this is one way to teach students there is another way to treat their fellow human beings. Students usually respond positively to courtesy from their teachers and often become more courteous in return.

Reward Small Achievements

14. Assign tasks according to each student's ability and interest level, making it possible for the student to gain positive reinforcement.

If the assigned task is at the underachiever's ability level (which could be higher or lower than the level of the class) and is something which he or she is interested in, the probability of success is much higher. This success, in turn, provides the opportunity for reinforcement and more success.

15. Relate successes to one another by telling a child about his past accomplishments and by relating strengths to future goals.

Many underachievers have no understanding that small accomplishments relate to one another and that all such accomplishments are steps toward a larger goal. As your underachieving students reach small goals, relate each to one another and to a larger goal ahead.

16. Emphasize those things that the student has learned, even if mistakes were made.

More learning can be gained from the mistakes one makes than from one's successes. Few students, however, understand this concept. When an underachiever makes mistakes, point out what has been learned from these mistakes rather than focusing on the mistakes themselves.

17. Genuinely accept each student, including the shortcomings or lack of skills that the underachieving student may have.

Underachievers often feel that they are not living up to the expectations of their parents and teachers, and therefore, that they are not accepted by these significant adults. If you genuinely accept underachieving students, a climate conducive to trust building will occur.

18. Share stories from your childhood which illustrate times when you made mistakes.

All of us have made mistakes, and most of the time we've learned from them. Hearing about your experiences will help students to accept their limitations along with their strengths. They realize that you are not perfect and that you don't expect them to be perfect, either.

19. Assign thought papers or journal writing.

Thought papers are written assignments on any personal topic the student chooses. They are to be ungraded and returned with personal notes within a day or two after they are turned in. Journals have a similar approach and function, but are usually ongoing over a period of time.

20. Use video journals for sharing feelings and building trust.

This is sometimes called the "confessional booth" approach. Give each student a blank videotape at the beginning of the school year or grading period. Set up a video camera in a private location such as a closet or small room. When any student feels like getting something off his chest or sharing a concern, he can take his videotape and record his thoughts. As trust builds, the tape can be shared with the teacher or can be used as a personal record of thoughts and feelings.

21. Conduct private, personal conferences with your underachievers while the rest of the class is doing something on their own.

Private time is invaluable in setting the stage to reverse underachievement. If possible, have a volunteer or paraprofessional watch the class while you are doing this so that you are able to give the student one-on-one personal attention. Take the time to share your own thoughts, opinions, and views.

22. Accept your underachiever's feelings about school or about life - even if you disagree with them.

Give your underachievers opportunities to express their points of view and acknowledge them, even when you do not agree with what they are saying. Feelings do not have right and wrong answers! Responding to feelings with "Don't feel like that!" isn't very helpful. Instead, accept feelings in a non evaluative manner. A feeling is not a behavior. Often we react to feelings as if they were behaviors instead of listening to and accepting them.

23. Be aware that underachievers can be manipulative. Do not allow them to use all of your time.

Many underachievers have learned to manipulate their parents and teachers in ways which give them more power than they should have. Building trust and acceptance is a two-way street. Be firm with underachieving students when they try to use or manipulate you.

24. Let students try things on their own.

It is very hard to give up some of the control and not micro manage your classroom. As trust grows with your underachievers, allow them to take some of the responsibility for their own learning. They will not always succeed, and in fact, they will not always respond to this type of treatment. But for some underachievers, this is a sign that you really do trust them to do what is right.

> *We are what we repeatedly do.*
> *Excellence is not an event. It is a habit.*
> *- Aristotle*

HELLPING STUDENTS IN SELF DISCOVERY

Successful Strategies . . .

Encourage and Facilitate Counseling and Sharing

25. Include activities which will help the student explore his/her attitudes, opinions and self awareness.

The emphasis in schools today seems focused on academic skills. Nevertheless, many students will never be successful students academically without help in learning who they are. Social studies, language arts, health, physical education and the arts are all subject areas which may lend themselves to student self discovery. Look for ways to help students in this way as you teach these content areas.

26. Make students aware of available counseling services.

Many students are not aware of the various counseling services which may be available to them. Make sure you know sources of counseling not only at school, but also through community agencies and religious organizations. You may want to compile a list of local resources for counseling.

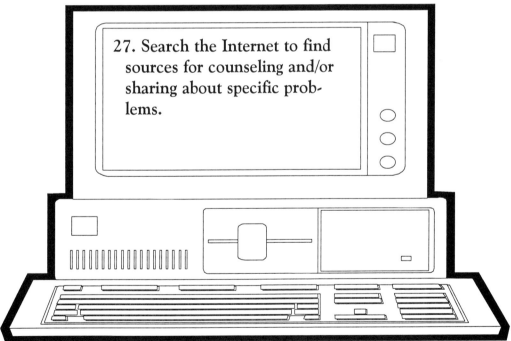

27. Search the Internet to find sources for counseling and/or sharing about specific problems.

The Internet has a wealth of resources and information available on almost any problem imaginable. Conduct a preliminary search for a student who has a specific concern or problem. Use your best judgment about appropriate sites. Check out your choices with your media specialist, district instructional technology personnel or school administrator. Encourage students to visit these sites to get more information or as a way to communicate with others.

28. Be open to opportunities for counseling your students, thereby becoming a catalyst for change.

The best counselor a student could have may be his or her classroom teacher. The classroom teacher often knows and understands the student much better than a counselor would, and the classroom teacher is in the perfect position to observe problems and frustrations first-hand. Teacher/student counseling relationships often develop naturally as a closeness develops during the course of the school year. As a classroom teacher, you probably will not be able to counsel each of your students individually, but you will be able to do this for some. Be open to such opportunities.

29. Recognize when the student needs more in-depth counseling than you can provide.

Often, well-meaning teachers end up in situations they do not have the training to deal with. Major depression, mental illness, addiction to drugs and alcohol, and serious family problems are examples of difficulties which may result in underachievement at school. It is important to help when you can, but equally important to know when you are beyond your level of expertise and that other professionals are needed to help with the problem.

30. Compare the child with himself, not with others.

The low self-esteem of underachievers often is exacerbated by competition and unfavorable comparisons to others. Such comparisons never reverse underachievement, and, in fact, may actually accelerate it if the child decides, "What's the use? I'm no good compared to the others anyway." On the other hand, showing an underachiever the progress he made by comparing what he is doing at the present time to what he was doing a week ago or a month ago is very helpful in keeping the momentum for achievement going. Parents must be particularly careful not to compare one sibling with another.

31. Find adults who were underachievers during their school years and who are now successful. How did they turn it around? Invite them to class and ask them to give their testimony.

A real life success story is worth a great deal. Choose your former underachievers carefully. Make sure that they value education, that they relate well to kids and that the reversal of their underachievement has application to the students you teach. If this is the case, such a testimony will have much value for your students.

32. Provide for a variety of good role models for your underachievers.

Investigate existing programs or begin a program such as Adopt-A-Grandparent, Big Brothers and Big Sisters, and Adult Mentors which pair successful, caring adults with children. Many such programs are available in most communities, but the teacher often has to find out about them and encourage the child to take part.

Help with Goal Setting

33. Help the student set goals, and assist him or her in seeing ways to achieve these goals.

Use the goal setting form on the next page or the goal setting web on the following page to guide your students as they set goals. The goal setting form works well with sequential learners; the web provides an opportunity for random thinkers to brainstorm all of the possible strategies for reaching a goal without deciding initially what they must do first. Written goals which are reassessed each grading period provide structure and a sense of direction for underachievers. Avoid goals which seem unattainable or ones that are only long term in nature.

34. Teach the problem solving method in order to engage the student in joint decision making on both academic and affective goals.

If your student has trouble setting goals, or if he or she cannot see how to go about achieving the goals that have been set, try the problem solving method. Using the problem solving forms on pages 28 and 29, engage in problem solving with an individual student or with a small group.

35. Give prompt feedback in assessing progress toward the goals.

The goal setting sheet on the next page is designed to be used in reassessing students at the end of each grading period. Use your best judgment in deciding if this is often enough. If not, adapt the form for more frequent use. Some underachievers require feedback on their progress once a week. Others can go longer. Do not allow more than nine weeks to go by without reassessment.

36. Be aware that academic goals, like personal goals, do not need to be the same for each student.

The present delivery system in American education is linked with student progress based on time and chronological age. In many cases, this model has not worked well, because it has made it difficult to plan for individual differences. As 21st century educators, we are rethinking the way we deliver educational services. We are developing strategies so that our students no longer need to be in a lock step pattern where everyone in the class learns the same thing at the same time. We are beginning to realize that students need choices and flexibility in their learning. Helping your students set appropriate individual academic goals is an important first step.

See Teaching Tools for the 21st Century by Carolyn Coil (Pieces of Learning, publisher) for information about how to design lessons and units of study which incorporate student choices as well as required activities.

GOAL SETTING

or . . .
WHERE DO YOU WANT TO GO
AND
HOW DO YOU PLAN TO GET THERE?

1. What school related goals would like to work toward during the next grading period?

a._____

b._____

c._____

During this school year?

a._____

b._____

After high school?

a._____

b._____

2. What personal goals would you like to achieve in the next six months?

a._____

b._____

c._____

Within the next year or two?

a._____

b._____

How do you expect to achieve you these goals?

a._____

b._____

c._____

a._____

b._____

a._____

b._____

How do you hope to achieve these goals?

a._____

b._____

c._____

a._____

b._____

Reproducible page for student use.

Mindmap - Problem Solving, Goal Setting & Decision Making

Complete the circles with your goal and steps to achieve it. Then number the circle
in the order you need to attack your goal.

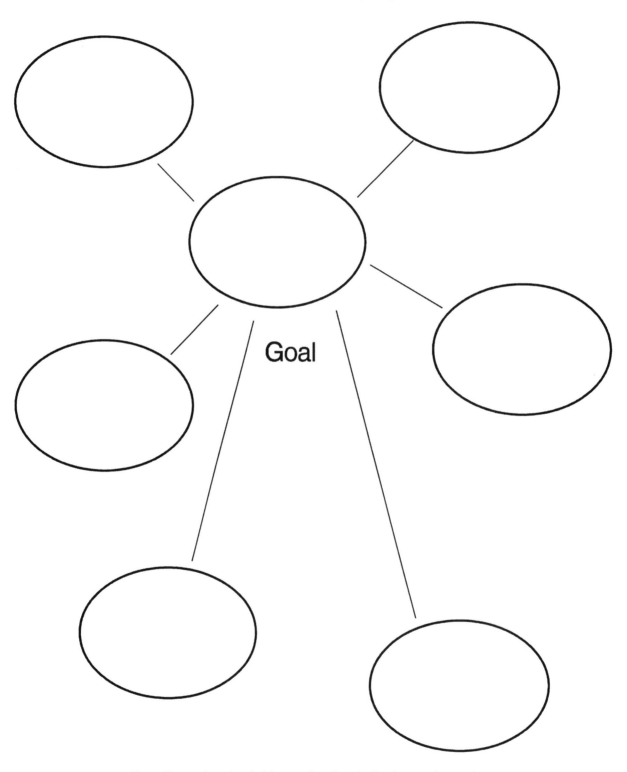

From **Becoming An Achiever**, Carolyn Coil, Pieces of Learning
Reproducible page for student use.

PROBLEM SOLVING FOR GOAL SETTING AND DECISION MAKING

Step 1: State the problem.

Step 2: With at least one other person, brainstorm possible solutions to the problem. Remember, in brainstorming all ideas are accepted!

IDEAS

1.____

2.____

3.____

4.____

5.____

6.____

7.____

8.____

Step 3: Now write some positive points and some negative points about the ideas listed. In your list of ideas (above) put + for each positive idea and - for each negative idea.

Step 4: In the space below, write down the ideas you will try and when you will try them.

IDEA	TIME LINE

Reproducible page for student use.

37. Talk about the future with your underachievers.

In an "instant gratification" culture, many students spend very little time thinking about the future except in a very general and unrealistic way. This is particularly true of underachievers who tend to think only of what they want today. Talking together can help them set realistic goals for academics, social life and athletics. Be sure to discuss their responsibilities and ways you may be able to help them reach their goals.

38. Introduce your students to the Lifeline Activity which shows how events of the past and present can point the way to the future.

To do this activity, give your students several index cards in each of three colors. For example, yellow cards can be used for past events and people, green for present day friends, activities, etc. and blue for hopes and dreams of the future. After the three sets of lifeline cards are completed, each student sorts his or her cards in a number of ways to identify challenges, see patterns from the past and present which give clues to future actions or decide which goals make the most sense to start working on first. This activity is a hands-on goal setting activity which fascinates and motivates many underachievers.

Use Peers and Small Group Activities

39. If the child is not accepted by his or her peers, encourage socialization within the class, particularly with an achieving peer.

Some underachievers have terrific social skills, but others do not fare very well socially. If you have an underachiever who is not accepted by the peer group, try pairing this student with an achiever of the same ability level who is also accepting, encouraging and friendly. Sometimes students who are paired in this way for a specific school project will develop a friendship which will be of immense benefit to the underachiever.

30 © 2001 Pieces of Learning

40. Teach social skills.

Feeling at ease in a variety of social situations with peers and with adults will enhance confidence and self-esteem. There are many social skills and rules of simple etiquette that are beneficial to know. If your underachievers do not have a natural social ability, knowing and practicing these skills greatly boosts self esteem.

41. Develop a system for peer tutoring.

A "study buddy" system works well for some underachievers. Achievers seem to form study groups without encouragement from parents and teachers. Such students study together on a routine basis throughout middle school, junior high and high school. Underachievers do not tend to form such groups on their own, but benefit greatly when they can work or study with another student.

42. Pair an underachiever with an achiever of approximately the same ability level.

This seems to be the best configuration when grouping underachievers in a classroom, work, or study environment. If an underachiever is grouped with two achieving peers, the underachiever will allow the achievers to do all the work! Conversely if two underachievers are grouped with one achiever, the achiever feels stressed and worries that no work will get done. In a traditional cooperative learning group, the underachiever usually feels that there are plenty of other people to do the work without him having to put forth much effort.

43. Use cell phones to set up a student homework hotline.

Get donations of cell phones and phone service from a business partner or wireless phone company. You could also write a grant to cover the cost of this program. Distribute the cell phones on a rotating basis to honor students in various subject areas. Publicize the numbers as a student homework hotline in the subject areas targeted. With this strategy, an underachiever could get help from an achieving peer in a more anonymous fashion and without looking like a nerd or social misfit! This strategy works best in high school but is also feasible with some middle school students.

44. Encourage students to reinforce each other when they do well.

Most American schools emphasize competition rather than cooperation between students. In a competitive atmosphere, there are always winners and losers. While this works well for the achieving winners, it can be devastating for the rest of the students. When it is workable within your classroom organization, create a climate of cooperation instead of competition. Positive reinforcement from peers is a powerful tool in bringing about achievement in students who normally are underachievers.

45. Ask your underachievers to be peer tutors in their areas of strength.

Underachievers have definite areas of strength (see Strategy 7). After you have identified these strengths. allow your underachievers to become peer tutors. Not only will this help them academically, but it will also give a boost in self confidence and self esteem.

46. Hold class meetings which are problem solving in nature.

In such meetings, the teacher serves as a facilitator. Ideas are put on the class agenda prior to the meeting. Discussions on the agenda topics are held with a time limit set for each topic. If a solution about a given topic is not reached within the time limit, a small group from the class brainstorms possible solutions to be discussed at the next class meeting.

47. Use cross-age tutors to help improve academic and social skills.

Using both underachieving and achieving students in a cross-age tutoring program is beneficial to both. Underachievers often shine when asked to help younger students with a skill they have mastered themselves. They also tend to respond favorably when they can be tutored by an older student, particularly one they perceive is "cool."

48. Teach conflict management skills.

Most students face a variety of conflict situations every day. They see conflict in their homes and neighborhoods and conflict between students at school. The evening news reports incidents of conflict daily, and unfortunately some of these are related directly to schools. Conflict has come to the forefront as an issue on everyone's mind. It is the rare student who does not have to manage conflict in some way. Underachievers may engage in conflict-producing activities as a way to avoid work. And like all students, they may worry about the possibility of an incident of severe conflict at home or at school. One thing we can do is deal with this issue in class. A lesson plan for introducing the topic is found on the next page.

INTRODUCING CONFLICT MANAGEMENT
A Lesson Plan for Grades 4-8

1. Definition:

On chart paper or the board, write the word CONFLICT. Have students brainstorm what they think it means. Write down their definitions beneath the word CONFLICT.

2. Compare and Contrast the Shades of Meaning:

Discuss the definitions the students have generated plus any of your own that have not been mentioned. Emphasize similarities and differences in the meanings.

3. Making a Continuum:

Draw a horizontal line the length of the board. Write *Less Severe* at the end of the line to the left, and *Most Severe* at the end of the line on the right. Divide the students into small groups. Ask each group to write each of the definitions where they think they should be placed on the continuum. Discuss the placements, having students from the different groups write the placement on the board. Talk about shades of meaning between the definitions and discuss why some conflicts are more severe than others.

4. Categorizing Types of Conflict:

Write each of these phrases on a piece of newsprint or overhead transparency:

> Conflict within yourself
> Conflict between groups of people in the same
> family/school/neighborhood/town/state/country
> Conflict between countries
> Conflict between ideas

Assign each small group a type of conflict. Have each group prepare and then perform a skit illustrating their type of conflict.

5. Discussion:

> Are conflicts ever worth having?
> When are they detrimental?
> When are they helpful?

> What conflicts do you worry most about?
> What are ways we could handle these conflicts in a positive manner?

Dispel the Fear of Failure

49. Help the student to set realistic expectations.

Some underachievers set no goals while others "dream the impossible dream," setting goals for themselves which can never be met. In either case, their expectations are unrealistic, and they set themselves up for failure. Helping students establish realistic goals which can be accomplished leads them to an experience of success, an important first step in dispelling the fear of failure.

50. Discourage the drive for perfection which cannot be met.

Some underachievers are perfectionists. When this is the case, it may seem easier to the student never to attempt a task rather than create something which is not perfect. A flexible classroom climate where less than perfect products are routinely accepted helps the perfectionist feel that his/her attempts have worth. Keeping high expectations for ones' students while encouraging discouraged perfectionists is a balancing act which requires teacher flexibility in establishing individualized assessment criteria for assigned work.

51. Encourage participation in class.

Students who are reluctant to participate in class may tell you that they don't want to be embarrassed. Most of the time, this is another way of saying that they are afraid of failure and are concerned about their classmates' reactions. If your underachiever is reluctant to participate, plan classroom activities which lend themselves to his/her strengths. Encourage the student's participation in these activities.

52. Discuss the worst case scenario and then go beyond it.

When presented with a new idea or task, many underachievers immediately think of the worst possible thing that could happen if they tried to do the task and didn't succeed! Encourage these students to verbalize or write out their worst case scenarios but don't stop there. Have students look at the end of their worst case scenario and then ask, "What would happen next?" This usually gives them a new perspective. Even if the worst thing happens (which it probably won't), life will go on, and eventually things will return to normal. This exercise helps them see that failure isn't the end of the world.

REMEMBER . . . Change takes place slowly over a long period of time and change is not easy. In most cases, low self esteem has developed over a number of years. It will not change overnight. But it is possible to change self concepts. Try some of the strategies that have been suggested in this chapter. Find the ones that are most successful for you and your students. And then give the strategies time to work. Over a period of a few weeks, you will see a difference!

Chapter 3

IMPROVING STUDY SKILLS
AND
REMEDIATING ACADEMIC WEAKNESSES

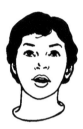

Jason is a sixth grader. He made it through elementary school getting Bs and Cs on his report card. His parents and teachers knew he could do better; he rarely studied in elementary school. At the beginning of the school year, he entered middle school. He was placed in an advanced class because he was considered to have high academic ability, but most of his teachers see gaps in the academic skills he has. He has problems writing his thoughts in complete sentences, doesn't know how to learn the scientific terminology being taught in science class, and fails math tests because he has gaps in his knowledge of computational facts. At the same time, he shines in class discussion, has advanced knowledge of current events and enjoys talking to his science teacher about conservation and the environment. When the first middle school report card was issued, Jason received Cs and Ds. He is an underachiever with some specific academic weaknesses. He also needs help in learning study skills. In order for him to succeed in school, these weaknesses must be remediated. At the same time, his motivation and interest must be sustained.

Most underachievers need to improve academic habits and develop better study skills. Underachievers (or potential underachievers) often breeze through the first few years of elementary school, putting forth little effort to study. The first signs of underachievement may appear when grades or achievement test scores fall slightly. While these students may be satisfied with their own performance, the end result is that they go through five or six years of school without developing any study skills or the tenacity and self discipline which usually accompanies them. At some point in every student's life, the time comes when he or she does not know the material being taught and can no longer breeze through without "cracking a book." It suddenly becomes apparent that studying is a necessity in order to do well.

Since this often happens during the middle school years, statistically underachievement seems to increase drastically between grades 5 - 8. The reason is not so much that adolescence has hit and teenage hormones are raging, though this certainly plays a role. More often than not, a child will put forth exactly the same amount of effort and continue using the same work habits as he or she had in earlier grades. The difference is that it is no longer possible to know all of the required content, remain organized in a number of different subjects taught by different teachers, and complete all of the long range assignments without having good academic and organizational habits, a time management plan, and appropriate study skills.

This chapter examines strategies that help underachievers improve their study skills and strategies that assist them in remediating specific academic weaknesses.

IMPROVING STUDY SKILLS

Successful Strategies . . .

Help Develop Organizational Skills

53. Talk to the student and his/her parents about ways to organize the study environment at home.

Parents are essential in helping to develop a plan for organized studying. Students need a specific place for study and a specific time set aside for this purpose. This should be done on a daily basis, whether or not the student has assigned homework. Homework supplies must be available and the environment must be conducive to study. Working with parents to achieve this is an important first step in developing an underachiever's study skills.

54. Encourage parents and students to organize the study area in a central location.

Homework is best done at a location near the rest of the family, usually the place where the family computer is located. Kids don't feel isolated or exiled and parents can keep an eye on organizational skills as well as homework and computer usage. This area should be reasonably quiet, well lit and the TV should not be on.

55. Design a class preparedness checklist, listing materials needed for your class.

Make a poster or bulletin board listing those items each student should have for your class. Review this list periodically, either with the entire class or with the underachievers who do not come to class prepared. Most teachers do this at the beginning of the school year, but for some students, a weekly or monthly reminder is helpful. The list may change during the school year; do not require students to bring items they will not use during a given week. For example, if you will not be using the textbook, tell them ahead of time.

56. Allow underachievers to keep a copy of the textbook at home and use another copy at school.

This strategy will work well if you happen to have extra textbooks. When this is the case, arrange for the parent to get the textbook and keep it in the study environment at home (see Strategy 53). When this strategy is used, the student ends up with fewer books to keep track of and finds it much easier to remain organized.

57. Assist your underachievers in developing an individual checklist of supplies.

Develop a checklist of supplies needed at home for doing homework and supplies needed in class at school. Such a list is best developed with the student or students involved. Help them think about those things they need on a routine basis at home and at school. The list then should be divided in half. The list of supplies needed at school should be taped to a door at home so it can be read and orally checked before the student leaves for school in the morning. Similarly, the list of supplies needed at home should be taped on the student's desk or locker for daily reference before leaving school for the day. It sometimes helps to compare this to an airline pilot who must go through the same checklist each time before a flight commences. A sample checklist is below.

School Supplies Checklist	
Supplies needed at school:	Supplies needed at home:
___Notebook paper	___Notebook paper
___2 pencils	___Pencil
___Pen	___Pen
___Text for each class	___Textbooks (which ones)
___Loose-leaf notebook	___Dictionary
___Graph paper	___Colored pencils
___Ruler	___Phone numbers of smart/responsible classmates
___Calculator	

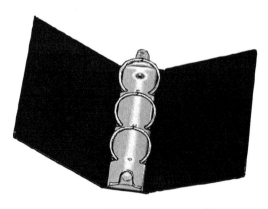

58. Suggest that your students carry a backpack, tote bag, or other container for carrying school materials.

Most achievers seem to automatically have the items which help in being an organized student. An essential is some type of carrier in which to place materials, books and supplies. The "in" thing changes from year to year, but the organizational function remains the same. Be sure you know your school's policy regarding appropriate types of book bags. Some school districts require see-through or net bags. Whatever the type, encourage all of your students to have something in which to put their supplies.

59. Give students a luggage tag to put on their book bags with a checklist of needed supplies on it.

In keeping with the airline theme (see Strategy 57), a luggage tag not only identifies whose bag is whose, but it also can serve a useful function of helping students organize supplies. A generic list can be printed and laminated, then given to each student in the form of a luggage tag.

60. Give positive reinforcement when the disorganized student brings appropriate supplies to class.

All students should come to class ready to learn and with appropriate supplies. This seemingly simple expectation is difficult for many underachievers to accomplish. Don't overlook this when it happens; positive reinforcement often leads to a repeat performance.

61. Teach students how to generate and use a daily or weekly "To Do List."

Like goal setting (see Strategies 33-38), daily or weekly planning is an undeveloped time management skill for most underachievers. Use the reproducible sheet on page 41 in helping students formulate a "To Do List." Assist them in scheduling those items on a daily or weekly basis. Often this works well in conjunction with learning to write down assignments (see Strategy 62).

62. Require that all students write down assignments.

An assignment sheet provides a way for students to record daily, weekly and long term assignments. A suggested format can be found on page 42. Some schools have agendas or other booklets which are supplied to the students. However, if your under-

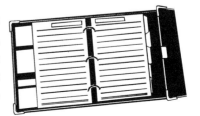

achievers balk at any of these, ask them to write the assignment on a self-stick note. Almost all will do this! Most then put the self-stick note on the book containing the assignment or on the sheet of paper the assignment needs to be done on. The 80-20 rule applies here. About 80% of what is written down actually gets done. For most underachievers, this is progress!

63. Use an "Assignments Completed" chart.

Design an "Assignments Completed" chart for your entire class or for specific individuals in your class. This type of chart lists all of the required assignments and provides a space to indicate when each has been completed and turned in. This chart does not reflect the quality of the product; its purpose is to help disorganized students see the large picture of what is required in a given class and measure how much he or she has accomplished. These are great for students to use when organizing their portfolios. A sample form can be found on page 43.

TO DO LIST

<u>Activity</u>   <u>When</u>

1._____   1._____

2._____   2._____

3._____   3._____

4._____   4._____

5._____   5._____

6._____   6._____

7._____   7._____

8._____   8._____

9._____   9._____

10._____   10._____

11._____   11._____

12._____   12._____

Reproducible page for student use.

ASSIGNMENTS

Today's Date: _____

Subject: _____

Assignment: _____

_____

Materials Needed: _____

_____

Due Tomorrow_____Due Next Week_____Due (Date)_____

Subject: _____

Assignment: _____

_____

Materials Needed: _____

_____

Due Tomorrow_____Due Next Week_____Due (Date)_____

Subject: _____

Assignment: _____

_____

Materials Needed: _____

_____

Due Tomorrow_____Due Next Week_____Due (Date)_____

Reproducible page for student use.

ASSIGNMENTS COMPLETED

Assignment Description	Date Completed	Date Turned In
1. _____	_____	_____
_____		
2. _____	_____	_____
_____		
3. _____	_____	_____
_____		
4. _____	_____	_____
_____		
5. _____	_____	_____
_____		
6. _____	_____	_____
_____		
7. _____	_____	_____
_____		
8. _____	_____	_____
_____		
9. _____	_____	_____
_____		

Reproducible page for student use.

64. Require your students to use loose leaf notebooks. Encourage the use of dividers for better organization.

The advantage of using loose leaf notebooks is that papers can be easily added, taken out, or rearranged. This is a great help to the disorganized student. Use dividers to separate subjects or to categorize information within one subject area. Underachievers who are aided in their organizational skills by being required to keep a notebook generally become much better organized as the school year progresses.

65. Make a schedule for checking student notebooks and stick with it.

A periodic check of notebooks will help you assess the organizational skills of your students and will encourage students to stay organized. When students know their notebooks will be checked on a regular basis, they are more likely to remain organized.

66. Reward students who have complete notebooks.

When you check student notebooks (see Strategy 65), allow those students whose notebooks are complete to do something special while the others organize the portions of their notebooks which are not complete. This will encourage some underachievers to organize their notebooks ahead of time and will give an opportunity for other students to get organized who would not do so otherwise.

67. Design a system whereby parents periodically check their child's notebook.

Work with parents of your underachievers to develop a schedule for notebook checks. Plan for the parents to check their child's notebook before they are checked in class (see Strategy 65). This increases the possibility that the child will be rewarded in class for having a completed notebook (see Strategy 66). Such success will encourage more success!

68. Assist students in previewing their textbook, workbooks, or other print resources you will be using in class on an ongoing basis.

The best time to teach students how to preview texts and other resources is at the beginning of the school year when the materials are new to them. Together, examine the layout of the books, seeing how chapters and units of study are divided, where questions are located and what type of questions they are, how pictures, graphs, maps are used, etc. If you can obtain any evaluation sheets from a textbook adoption committee, these provide excellent guidelines for textbook preview. Discuss the pace at which you hope to go through the text and workbooks and how you will use the other print resources. Taking time for this preview will be helpful in giving many of your underachievers the "whole picture" for your class for the year. This is a great strategy for global learners.

69. Show students how to paraphrase the main ideas in the text and turn those ideas into questions.

Help your underachievers practice finding the main ideas in their textbooks, writing them down, and making them into questions. This is best done in teams with a game format. Once the questions are written, teams compete to see which team can answer another team's questions.

70. Have students develop their own study guides for each chapter they are studying.

When individual study guides are completed, group students together to compare their study guides for the same chapter. Offer suggestions for items they may have omitted or overlooked. This teaches how to extract important information from a textbook chapter and is more effective in the long run than doing a study guide for them. It also helps motivate students as they see they have the ability to find the important information on their own.

71. Have your students write memos to their textbook authors.

After completing a chapter or unit of study, have each student write a memo to the authors of the textbook explaining what he or she understood and didn't understand, what was meaningful and what was not. It is motivating to the students to write the memo, and it helps them read more carefully and go beyond the factual knowledge to a deeper understanding of what is being conveyed. Assign one student per chapter to write a cover letter and send all the student memos to the textbook publisher.

72. Show your students how to scan print material when they need to answer specific questions or find specific information or terms.

Underachievers are the first ones to say: "I couldn't find the answer to that question. It wasn't in the book" or "I couldn't find the definitions to any of the vocabulary words." While these statements are often weak excuses for laziness, underachievers respond when they learn how to scan material quickly. Practice scanning print material with your whole class or with a small group by having a contest and timing students to see how fast they can find specific items.

73. Have an uninterrupted morning literacy block.

No assemblies, PA announcements, or other interruptions are allowed during this time. This intensive and intentional use of time for literacy improves achievement for almost all children, including underachievers.

74. Develop techniques for building vocabulary, especially vocabulary in specific content areas.

Show your students how vocabulary words are most often delineated in their text. Some books use italics, some underline, some use bold print, some use a combination of techniques. Once the words have been identified in some way, the simple index card is one of the best tools to assist students in learning vocabulary. Instruct your students to write the word on one side and the definition on the other. Write examples or mnemonic tricks for learning the word. Use the cards for individual review or for drill and practice activities in pairs or small groups.

75. Use word walls to help students learn new vocabulary.

Research in brain-based learning suggests a print rich environment helps develop and build reading skills. Cover at least one wall in your classroom with words, especially new vocabulary words, or words that are related to a current unit of study. Some underachievers will be motivated to add words to the wall which will challenge other students. Underachievers also benefit from being able to refer to the word wall when they want to improve their writing or their vocabulary but don't want to ask for help.

76. Teach required novels or short stories through drama and graffiti.

Break the novel up into smaller segments, like acts and scenes in a play. Assign speaking parts to some students with others taking the part of the narrator. Use costumes and props as the novels are being read. At the end of each class period, have your students write notes about what they remember from the day on large pieces of chart paper or on mural paper which have been placed around the classroom. These should be written in the same way they might write graffiti. Use these as review notes at the end of the novel.

77. Use the "Speed System" in teaching active reading.

Many students are interested in cars, particularly in how fast they go. Tap into this interest by comparing the various speeds appropriate to use when driving a car with the various speeds appropriate to use when doing assigned reading. Give your students a copy of the reproducible page "What's the Right Speed" and go over it with them. Then be very specific when you tell your students to read something. If you use the "Speed System" you can give reading assignments like this:

Tonight I want you to read pages 34-50 like Speed Demons. Look for ten new vocabulary words as you read and write them down.

or

Now you need to distinguish between the facts and the opinions in what we've been studying. When you read, read the same material several times just like you drive around the same area several times when you're Cruisin' Through McDonald's®.

This system helps underachievers to know exactly what is expected of them when the teacher says, "I want you to read . . ."

WHAT'S THE RIGHT SPEED . . .
How Fast Should You Read?

Like driving, reading is done at different speeds, depending on the circumstances.

"Speed Demon" (Skimming) *1000 - 2000 words per minute*

- To locate a specific reference or vocabulary word
- To find the answer to a specific question
- To get a general overview of a chapter, short story or article

"Interstate Travel" (Rapid Reading) *500 - 1000 words per minute*

- To review something you have already read
- To read magazines, comic books, or feature articles in newspapers
- To read for pleasure, for example an easy novel

"Driving in Town" (Moderate Reading with Pauses as Needed)
350 - 500 words per minute

Fiction:
- To read fiction that is somewhat difficult
- To read for characterization, theme, mood, imagery, etc.

Non-Fiction:
- To find the main idea and make generalizations
- To understand patterns and sequence

"Cruisin' Through McDonald's®" (Reading the Same Material Several Times) *250 - 350 words per minute*

Fiction:
- To read complex fiction for characterization and plot analysis; to understand relationships between characters and ideas

Non-Fiction:
between
- To note details, compare and contrast information, distinguish

fact and opinion

"Speed Bumps" (Slow Reading) *50 - 250 words per minute*

Fiction:
- To evaluate quality and literary merit
- To study and master content, including facts and details
- To learn new vocabulary and literary style

Non-Fiction:
- To read technical or scientific material
- To solve a complex problem
- To follow detailed directions

Both:
- Translating from another language

Reproducible page for student use.

78. Promote a love of reading.

Any reading that is done on a student's own time will result in his or her achievement scores going up. This is true for all types of achievement tests and for the verbal portion of the SAT. There are many ways to promote reading; several suggestions are listed below. Find at least one that works for you. Readers become achievers!

*Get every student a library card.

*Go to the library for a field trip.

*Connect reading assignments to students' real world experiences.

*Reserve a portion of your classroom time for free reading.

*Work with your school administration to set aside time during the week when everyone in the school reads.

*Investigate a business partnership which will provide reward or incentives to students who read.

*Challenge your students to read a certain number of pages and chart each student's progress.

Help Develop Listening Skills

Juan is an average 7th grade student whose achievement tests indicate that he should be doing much better than he is. When he began junior high, he realized that he couldn't remember all of the information the teachers gave verbally during lectures and class discussions. He talked to his friends about it to see if they were having the same problem. Some of them said they took notes during class and reminded Juan that the teachers had talked to them about notetaking.

"How can I listen and write at the same time?" Juan asked. "Besides, I don't know what to write. It's impossible to write down everything they say!"

Juan could become an achiever if he developed good listening and notetaking skills.

Use Helpful Lecturing Techniques

79. Teach students to know the differences between important and irrelevant information.

Underachievers often have difficulty distinguishing between verbal information which is important to remember and information which is irrelevant or is just given as an example. Emphasize your most important points to help focus your students (see Strategy 80).

80. Emphasize main points and supporting details.

An achieving student soon learns not only how to distinguish the main points of the lecture, but also important details. Underachievers have difficulty with this skill. Emphasize not only your main points but also those details and facts which your students will need to know to do well on written work and tests.

81. Provide an outline of important lecture points.

An outline of the important points in your lecture can be invaluable to the student who has difficulty with listening and notetaking skills. Because listening is a skill most easily learned by the auditory learner, visual learners will benefit most from a written outline.

82. Teach the art of verbal paraphrase.

When you read or lecture to your students, when they listen to another classmate or when they view a video or listen to a guest speaker, ask them to orally paraphrase and summarize what they have heard. This increases vocabulary and encourages active listening.

83. Repeat important points.

An old saying states: "Tell them what you're going to tell them, then tell them, and finally tell them what you've told them." This is a good formula to use when lecturing. Make sure you know exactly what points you want to emphasize, and repeat them several times. Students with poor listening skills have the most trouble learning from teachers who are disorganized or who ramble and digress while lecturing.

84. Teach students to identify verbal and nonverbal cues in order to recognize what information is important.

Most teachers develop a distinct lecturing style. Evaluate your lecturing techniques to discover the verbal and nonverbal cues you normally give when emphasizing important points. Discuss these with your students and have them add any of your pet phrases to the list of 'How to tell what is important' in the handout on page 55.

85. Show students how to take notes using a mindmap, concept map or web.

Using an outline is only one way to take good notes. Mapping instead of outlining is particularly helpful for visual learners and those who think in a random manner rather than in a linear sequential way. Underachievers who like to doodle while listening benefit greatly from this strategy.

Create Interest in Your Topic

86. Paint a verbal picture to help the student remember and understand the information.

Most factual information can be presented either in a dry, formal way or with stories, examples and descriptions which help students to visualize the information. Whenever possible, create interest in what you are saying by painting a verbal picture for your students. Enthusiasm is the key to helping your subject become alive for your students.

87. Help your underachievers relate new ideas to personal experiences.

New ideas and concepts are more interesting to anyone when they are related to one's self in a personal way. Students who do not have the intrinsic motivation to achieve are more likely to understand and remember facts and concepts when they are directly related to something he or she has personally experienced. Use interest inventories or informal autobiographies to learn about the personal interests and experiences of your students and relate what you are teaching to them whenever possible.

88. Demonstrate or illustrate important points in the lecture.

We live in an age where sophisticated visual presentations are commonplace. Therefore, hands-on demonstrations, illustrations and multimedia presentations, are often necessary to create interest in your topic. Underachievers who show little interest in a lecture become much more interested when they can see or participate in a demonstration or when the topic is presented through the use of technology.

89. Include an element of surprise when you are lecturing.

Many students classify teacher lectures as "boring," which in turn is an attitude which leads to underachievement. Successful lecturers plan on doing something unexpected at some point during their lecture time. Students pay attention to what is being said because they are looking for the element of surprise. Think of ways to surprise your students on class lecture days.

90. Pace your lectures to students, observing when their interest or attention span will not take any more talking.

The average attention span of today's student is shorter than the student of a generation ago. Our world is moving at a faster pace, television is full of "sound bites," and computer software and the Internet allow students to change focus with the click of a mouse. All of us are bombarded by constant information overload. Be aware of this as you lecture to your students. When their attention begins to wane, change your pace, change the activity, or change their physical position. Your awareness of and sensitivity to your students will be of particular help to your underachievers.

Help Students Practice Notetaking Skills

91. Teach your students how to note key terms.

Learning important vocabulary is essential for achievement in any subject area. Teaching your underachievers to find, write down, or take notes about key terminology and meanings is a basic step in showing them good notetaking skills.

92. Write key words as they are spoken.

An effective way for students to learn key terms (see Strategy 91) is for the teacher to write key words on the chalkboard, overhead transparency, or poster board while he or she is lecturing. This is more effective than having an entire list of words written on the board or on a worksheet beforehand.

93. Pre-teach difficult vocabulary and concepts.

In conjunction with the practice of writing key words (see Strategy 92), difficult vocabulary and concepts should be taught before the content of the lesson is introduced. When the student hears them during the lesson itself, they will be somewhat familiar with the terms.

94. Encourage the use of highlighter pens.

A number of commercially produced highlighter pens are available for student use. Color coding, highlighting important facts or dates, and rereading notes while highlighting the most essential information are a few of the uses for these pens. Highlighters help underachievers to focus, particularly kinesthetic learners who need something active to do as they learn. Using highlighters helps them review important information. Use different colors to highlight information. (Yellow = ideas; Blue = vocabulary; Green = important dates; Orange = important people)

95. Use the reproducible handout, "Taking Notes from Class Lectures" on the next page to review good notetaking skills with your students.

In general, underachievers have poor notetaking skills. Use this reproducible page to review the basic skills of notetaking with your underachievers.

TAKING NOTES FROM CLASS LECTURES

Pointers for Students

1. Come to class prepared.

   Look over other class notes and read the assigned textbook pages. The lecture will make much more sense if you have some background about what is being said. Determine how today's lecture relates to what was said yesterday.

2. Concentrate on what is being said not how it is said or who is saying it.

   Even a teacher you dislike may have valuable information to give to you!

3. Keep mentally and physically alert.

   Get enough sleep and eat breakfast before coming to school.

4. Listen, think and write.

   You can do all three of these at the same time! Most teachers speak at the rate of approximately 100 words per minute. Most people can think at about 400 words per minute. Use the time to think about what is really important to write down.

5. Try to focus on the main idea.

   What seems to be the main point or points the teacher tries to get across?

6. Write the teacher's examples in your notes.

   Examples often turn into test items.

7. Ask yourself, "What would I ask on a test from this information?"

   Write your sample test questions at the end of your notes.

8. Make a list, highlight or underline things the teacher said that were completely new.

   These are the things you will have to review and learn, because you don't already know them.

TAKING NOTES FROM CLASS LECTURES

Pointers for Students

How to tell what is important:

* You can tell that something is important when the teacher:

- Changes his/her tone of voice

- Puts something on the chalkboard

- Uses an illustration or example

- Gives you a formula or diagram

- Pauses so that you have time to write

- Repeats the same point

- Slows down for emphasis

* You can tell that something is important when the teacher says:

- Note this

- The (four) main points are . . .

- This is important.

- You'll probably see this again.

- Make sure you remember this.

- This type of thing is on the (SAT, Achievement Test, etc.)

- Your teacher's favorite phrase:

Help Students Complete Long Term Assignments

96. Provide a written checklist outlining the expectations and schedule for any long term assignment.

A checklist of this type is very helpful to underachievers who have poor planning skills because it breaks the long term assignment into smaller, doable segments. A suggested format can be found on the next page.

97. Break the assignment into smaller parts and have the student turn in each of the smaller parts on a set schedule.

Some underachievers are overwhelmed by large long range projects and do not have the organizational or planning ability to do them. For such students, it is more effective to break the assignment into its smaller component parts (see Strategy 96) and set a due date for each part. In the course of working with these students over a school year, the component parts can be increased in size so that skill is developed in doing long range assignments and turning in the entire assignment upon completion.

98. Provide a list of suggested resources and materials needed for the project.

A recommended list of resources, including books, other print materials, web sites, software, human resources, plus any physical materials needed for hands-on projects is helpful. Suggestions as to where these resources and materials can be found inexpensively will help your students and their parents.

99. State the final goal or outcome. Link it to the required activities the student will need to do in order to complete an assigned report or project.

Make sure you are explicit in stating your expectations of the outcome of the project. Underachievers do better when outcomes are concrete, not abstract, and when the teacher is clear about exactly what the assessment criteria are. Too much flexibility in the assignment without concrete suggestions and expectations generally is not helpful to underachieving students.

100. Use direct teaching to teach skills in:
Finding appropriate resources
Outlining
Notetaking
Writing bibliography and footnotes
Writing a rough draft
Proofreading
Writing the final report

Don't assume that your students know how to do these things or that these are skills to be taught just in English class. Teach each of these skills when you assign a long-range written report in any subject area.

LONG RANGE ASSIGNMENT PLANNING GUIDE

<u>Topic/Project:</u> _____

<u>Expectations/Criteria:</u>

<u>Steps to Completion</u>	<u>Target Date</u>
<u>1.</u>	
<u>2.</u>	
<u>3.</u>	
<u>4.</u>	
<u>5.</u>	
<u>6.</u>	
<u>7.</u>	
<u>8.</u>	

<u>Resources:</u>

Reproducible page for student use.

Help Develop Test Taking Skills

Maria is an eighth grader who is an underachiever because of her poor performance on tests. Her homework papers are done neatly and correctly, and Maria regularly contributes insightful ideas to class discussions. She tends to be a perfectionist and puts a great deal of pressure on herself to do well in school. However, her test grades generally range between 60-70%. In observing her during tests, one can see that she is very nervous, and when she receives poor grades on test papers, she is visibly upset. Maria is potentially an excellent student who suffers from test anxiety and has not developed any test taking skills.

Test Anxiety

101. Discuss test anxiety and what causes it with your students.

Most students have never heard of test anxiety, but more than 25% of them have it to some extent. Physical symptoms such as sweaty hands, rapid breathing, or mild stomach upset are common in students who have test anxiety. Test anxiety causes mental blocks about information one knows. Relaxation techniques can help. The basic causes of this syndrome are a lack of self confidence, an inability to study correctly and poor time management while taking tests.

102. Assess which students have test anxiety.

A quick assessment tool is "A Test About Tests," a reproducible handout found on the next page. Your students will be surprised to see where they stand in terms of test anxiety. This provides some students with great insight about their study habits, their self confidence, and the level of stress in their lives. It also gives the teacher important information about which students have test anxiety.

103. Work with students who have test anxiety on techniques to overcome it.

Test anxiety can be alleviated by first identifying and defining it. Then it is helpful to find ways to use stress reduction and relaxation techniques, build self confidence especially under times of pressure, and learn a variety of study skills and techniques. Many of the strategies discussed in this book will help in reducing test anxiety.

A TEST ABOUT TESTS

Name_____

Scoring: *4 - This describes me exactly.*
            3 - This describes the way I usually feel.
            2 - Sometimes I feel like this.
            1 - I rarely feel this way.
            0 - I have never felt like this.

_____1. I never feel prepared when I take a test.

_____2. I start to feel physically nervous and stressed before a test is given.

_____3. I can guarantee that I will not do well on any test I take.

_____4. The computerized test answer sheets tend to confuse me.

_____5. When I come across a question that I don't know, I panic.

_____6. I panic when others finish a test before I do, even if it's not a timed test.

_____7. I have mental blocks when I am taking a test.

_____8. I worry that I will run out of time during a timed test.

_____9. I look around the room and feel that everyone else taking the test knows more than I do.

_____10. The word "test" makes me panic.   TOTAL

Score Interpretation:

40-31. You suffer from major test anxiety. Stress reduction techniques, a time   m a n - agement plan, working to build your self-confidence, and learning a variety of study skills will help.

30-21. You have problems in test taking which are due to test anxiety. Relaxation techniques before a test and using a variety of study skills will help.

20-11. You are usually relaxed in your approach to test taking. It would be helpful to pin- point any items above in which you scored a 3 or 4. Work to improve in these areas.

10 or Below   You have no test anxiety!

Reproducible page for student use.

Memorization Techniques

104. Relate the facts to be memorized to something the student already knows.

Anything is easier to learn when it can be related to something one already knows. In teaching memorization techniques to students, the relationship can be very obvious or it can be a "force fit." Sometimes, thinking of one thing in relationship to something else to which it is not actually related is very humorous. The humor then provides the context in which the memorization takes place.

105. Teach your underachievers how to use a variety of mnemonic devices. Some of these are listed below. You may know of many others.

- Use acronyms. For example, make a word or phrase from the first letter of each term to be learned.

- Make up a rhyme, rap, song or poem containing the information one needs to learn.

- Provide concrete examples in order to remember abstract ideas.

- Use drawings and doodles as reminders of abstract concepts.

- "Location" Method: Picture terms to be remembered on objects in a familiar room. To remember the terms, mentally walk around the room, locating them one by one.

106. Help students organize information into categories.

It is easier for all of us to remember small pieces of information when they are placed in a larger category. We can, generally, remember seven to ten items. (That's why most of us can remember our phone numbers, social security numbers and even our extended zip codes!) Use diagrams, charts, flow charts and mapping techniques to show students visual organizational patterns (see Strategy 135).

107. Provide a study guide.

Many underachievers have difficulty pinpointing the most important concepts and facts in a given lesson. Providing an outline or study guide will help them to know which things are the most important.

108. Encourage students to put the main ideas or concepts they need to learn on index cards.

Have students write the main idea or concept on one side of the card and supporting facts on the other. This helps students to organize information (see Strategy 106). Have them arrange the cards in categories to facilitate memorization.

109. Have your students survey teachers or highly achieving students to find out what their favorite memory techniques are.

A very enjoyable strategy for underachievers, this survey can also help in teaching research skills (see Strategy 100). Learning techniques for memorization from their peers is a particularly successful technique to use with underachievers who have achieving friends.

110. Integrate important things to memorize into songs and teach them to your students.

There's a powerful link between music and memory! Notice how you remember the words to that popular song from your teenage years even if you haven't heard it since you were in high school. Almost anything can be memorized if it is put to music. Additionally, kids in general are motivated by music. If you are too embarrassed to sing to your students, have them make up the songs with the information in them and sing them to you. This strategy works with raps and poems as well as with songs.

111. Repeat key concepts each day.

Daily repetition of important information is a key to building long term memory. Even if the kids begin repeating the concepts back to you as you say them — telling you "We already know this!" — you will be sure that the concepts are in their long term memories. Don't overdo this strategy, but for essential concepts it works well.

112. Use one color of paper for all the handouts related to a specific unit of study.

This helps underachievers with organization and also with memory. It helps when you say, "I want you to remember the important information on the yellow sheets of paper."

Test Taking Hints

113. Distribute the "Test Taking Hints" reproducible handouts found on the following pages.

Use each handout to discuss specific test taking skills with your students.

Test Taking Hints for Students
Time Management

1. Look over the entire exam first. Note the number of sections. Notice how many questions are on the test and how long you have to take the test. Then figure out how long you have to complete each question. Try to adjust your speed to match the time allotted for the questions.

2. Take into account the weighting or number of points each item or section of the test is worth.

3. Bring a watch to help you keep track of the time and judge your tempo as you take the exam. You may need to adjust your speed.

4. Don't spend too much time on any one item. If you can't decide between two or three choices, go ahead and choose one. If there is no penalty for guessing, this is always the best approach. Mark the question on your paper in some way if you think you might want to go back to it if you have time.

5. Do not rush to get through the test. Use all the time you are given. There are no extra points given for being the first to finish!

6. On tests where you are not penalized for guessing, when you see your time is almost up and you have not answered all of the questions, fill in answers randomly for all of the unanswered questions. You will not have time to read the questions when you do this, but guessing at random is better than choosing no answer at all.

NOTES

Test Taking Hints for Students
Making Correct Choices

Following Directions

1. Listen carefully if directions are given orally.

2. Look for key words in the directions.

3. Make sure you know exactly how your answers are to be recorded.

4. Pay attention to the sample item or items in the directions.

5. Follow all written and oral directions for taking the test and marking the answer sheet.

Reading the Questions

1. Ask yourself:*
- What is this question really asking?
- Are there any key words?
- How would I ask this question in my own words?
- How would I answer this question in my own words?

*Note: It is particularly important to go through this process with difficult questions.

2. Don't read things into the questions that aren't there.

3. Don't make assumptions about details that are not stated.

4. Be aware of your own biases. Do not base your answers solely on your personal beliefs or experiences.

5. Use your best logical reasoning and general knowledge.

NOTES

Reproducible page for student use.

Test Taking Hints for Students
Making Correct Choices

Considering Multiple Choice Answers

1. Read each question carefully and consider all the choices. If more than one answer seems correct, choose the best answer.

2. When three of the answers are very similar in meaning, the other answer is usually the correct one.

3. When all of the answers are correct, choose the answer that includes all of the others.

4. If all of the answers except one seem correct, reread the beginning of the question. It may be asking for "all of these EXCEPT the following."

5. If an answer has more than one part, look for parts that are incorrect. If one part is incorrect, the entire answer is incorrect.

6. Formulate an answer before reading the choices. Then ask:
- Is there an answer similar to the one I thought of?
- Is this the best answer of the choices given?

7. Some answers will seem incorrect, irrelevant, ridiculous, too general or too limited. Eliminate these first and you will have less possible answers from which to choose.

Considering Grammar and Wording

1. Look for key words such as all, never, only, no, none, always. These words usually make the statement false. Key words such as somewhat, usually, and sometimes generally make the statement true.

2. Use clues such as verb tense and the use of "an" or "a" to reduce possible answers and save time. If the grammar in the question does not match the grammar in the answer, that answer is incorrect.

3. Look for words in the answers that are similar to the words in the question.

4. Look for key words in the question that tell you exactly the kind of answer that is called for.

5. Watch for chances to use information given in one question as clues to the answer to another question.

Reproducible page for student use.

Test Taking Hints for Students Taking Essay Exams

1. Budget your time. If there is more than one question, you will have to decide ahead of time how long to spend on each. Plan how much time you need to write each answer.

2. Think through what you are going to write before you begin. Outline your main points and jot down key words or phrases before you begin.

3. Begin by writing in general terms and then back up what you say by providing examples.

4. Begin a new paragraph for each main idea. Use your outline as a guide.

5. No matter what subject the essay exam is being written for, observe the rules of correct English usage. Therefore, when you have finished writing, it is important to proofread your answers. Check for:

- Lack of clarity
    Are there any sentences in which your ideas seem muddled?

- False statements
    Did you write anything you know is not true or correct?

- Statements which are too vague or have no meaning
    Are there phrases or sentences that you included just to fill space that really add nothing to what you are saying?

- Incorrect sentence structure
    Do you have run-on sentences or phrases which are misplaced?

- Omitted or misspelled words
    Check each word carefully. It is easy to leave out an important word when you are writing quickly! If a word looks wrong, try spelling it another way.

- Incorrect grammar
    Do your verbs agree with your subjects? Have you used pronouns correctly?

- Errors in punctuation
    Does every sentence have a question mark, period or exclamation mark at the end? Are your commas in the right place? Are you using commas where periods should go?

REMEDIATING ACADEMIC WEAKNESSES

Robbie has made it to fifth grade, but sometimes he feels lost in class. The worst time of the day is during math. The teacher thinks he should be working on decimals and division of fractions. The problem is that Robbie really doesn't know his multiplication facts very well, especially the 7s, 8s and 9s. His teacher believes he is intelligent and should be doing well in math, but each day he falls further and further behind. Robbie has a great sense of humor and a lot of his friends are in his class, so he clowns around a lot. His teacher has started thinking of him as a behavior problem.

Too often the assumption is made that underachieving students know the skills. However, often they do not know some of the basics. Such cases need assessment and remediation of academic weaknesses.

Successful Strategies . . .

Assess Skill Levels

114. Find assessment instruments that will pinpoint which skills students already know and which skills they need to be taught directly.

Standardized test scores will give you a place to begin in assessing skills. When you find an area of weakness, use an assessment instrument that will pinpoint exactly which skills are deficient. Often underachievers will have small gaps within skill areas and will resist when remediation is required for the entire skill area. They are more open to remediation when they are shown exactly what specific skills they need to work on and why.

115. Re-evaluate the underachieving student's skills and abilities often.

Many underachievers are quick learners. If you are remediating assessed deficits, be sure to reevaluate the student at regular intervals. Re-evaluation serves as a motivator and shows definitive progress in specific skill areas. With regular reassessment, the underachiever is encouraged to achieve in improving his or her skill levels. Use these assessments to show student progress, but do not use the scores as part of their grade.

116. Give your underachievers opportunities to compact the curriculum in their areas of strength.

Curriculum compacting is the process by which students are pre-assessed before a skill or series of skills are taught. Those who already know the skill or skills are allowed to document their mastery and "test out" of the regular classroom work. Compacting students are allowed to work on an alternate activity, usually a learning activity they have chosen. This strategy is a great motivator for underachievers who hate doing drill and practice in skills they already know.

Help Develop Needed Skills

117. When specific skills and gaps that need to be remediated are identified, plan an individualized program to work on them.

Find materials for your underachievers that will remediate specific skill areas. Individualized instruction is one option. Plan such instruction in such a way that these students will be exempt from other work while they are working to remediate specific skills. Most underachievers will not cooperate if they view remedial work as something they have to do in addition to all of their other work. They usually will cooperate when it can be done instead of other work.

118. Use materials on the student's skill level when teaching content skills.

Ask a special education teacher for help in finding appropriate materials. Your underachievers will need to learn content area skills. Remedial materials in all content areas are available to help students with skill deficits.

119. Pair an underachiever with a peer who understands the skill being taught.

Identify another student who has mastered the skill your underachiever is lacking. Pair these students with the explicit purpose of working on the skill. This is particularly effective when the achiever and under-achiever are of approximately the same ability level but the underachiever lacks a specific skill.

120. Have a debriefing session with your students after a major exam.

It has often been said that we can learn more from our mistakes than our successes. Use major exams as teaching tools. Offer the option of letting students retake the exam after you have gone over the answers; then average the two scores.

121. Help underachievers improve in their presentation of their products and written work.

Any marketing expert will tell you that packaging is important! If a student's writing is difficult to decipher, save one of his or her papers for two weeks and then give it back, asking the student to proofread it or read it to you. This will increase the student's awareness of ways he or she can improve in writing. Have students evaluate their own work in terms of how it looks and how it is presented, including which parts of the work are appealing and which parts need improvement.

122. Make sure your underachievers receive positive reinforcement while they are working to remediate skills.

Assign tasks according to each student's ability level, adjusting your academic standards so that all children will receive some type of positive reinforcement. Positive reinforcement motivates; negative criticism and punishment do not!

123. Work with your underachievers to stabilize grades that show a pattern of dropping. Then help them to raise their grades one subject at a time.

If all of a student's grades go down at the same time, first help to stabilize them so that they don't continue in a downward spiral. Once the grades are stabilized, then work with the student to bring up his or her grades in one or two subjects at a time. This makes the goal less overwhelming and more in the realm of possibility for the student.

124. Don't ignore the beginnings of a pattern of underachievement in your students.

The pattern of underachievement begins as early as third grade and symptoms of potential underachievement can start even sooner. The most effective treatments are prevention and early intervention. If you notice a drop in report card grades or standardized achievement test scores, a change in attitude or motivation regarding schoolwork, or the beginnings of behavior problems in a previously achieving student, use some of the strategies suggested in this book to prevent the underachievement from becoming worse.

125. Initiate testing to determine if your underachievers have learning disabilities.

One cause of underachievement is the presence of a learning disability. If you notice a need for remediation or definite gaps and deficits in specific skills, refer the student for further testing to see if he or she has a learning disability.

Work With Other Teachers

126. If the student is having problems in a class other than yours, have him/her bring assignments from other classes and offer assistance.

If you have developed a good relationship with an underachieving student and understand his/her skill deficits, encourage this student to bring assignments from other classes to you and offer your help. Use this strategy selectively; it will not be appropriate for every underachiever or for every class. However, it works well if you and the student can decide on a convenient time to work together and if the student is willing and motivated to improve.

127. Work with the other teachers to understand what the student needs to do and what his/her problem(s) are.

If you work in a teaching team, you are probably already using this strategy. If your school is not set up in teaching teams, make an effort to work with other teachers to pinpoint problems of underachievers and brainstorm solutions together.

128. Investigate the possibility of allowing the underachiever to change from one teacher to another if there is a personality clash.

Sometimes students are sporadic underachievers; that is, they achieve well for some teachers but perform poorly for others. If you see this pattern with any of your underachieving students, ask the guidance counselor or school administrator to consider a change in teachers for this student. In some school situations this is a possibility and in others it is not. Be cognizant that if a major personality clash between a student and teacher exists, this strategy may solve the student's underachievement problem.

129. Be sensitive to the needs of underachievers who leave your classroom to go to another teacher for a "pull-out" program.

Students who go to another classroom for any kind of a pull-out program can easily get behind in their regular classroom work. Collaborate with other teachers in planning. Help those students who leave your room for a portion of the day to stay caught up with their work. This is especially important with underachievers who have poor organizational skills.

Teach Content-Specific Vocabulary

130. Find out which of the content vocabulary words your students already know and relate new vocabulary to these terms.

Vocabulary is the key to understanding the basic concepts in most subject areas. This is especially true in literature, the sciences and social studies. Usually, students will have some general knowledge about the topic and therefore will know some of the basic vocabulary. Build on this knowledge in teaching new words and terminology. Choose your vocabulary words carefully. Do not require students to learn an extraordinary number of difficult, technical words!

131. Have a class discussion using the vocabulary of your content unit.

Use new words in class conversation. Many times underachievers will demonstrate through discussion that they know much more than will show up in a paper/pencil assessment.

132. Use word puzzles to teach vocabulary.

Word puzzles are enjoyable, educational and motivating for many students. Use them as a means of introducing or reviewing vocabulary terms. Many publishers include word puzzles in their materials. Additionally, inexpensive computer software is available that allows you to create your own word puzzles.

133. Develop stories using vocabulary words.

Use vocabulary words to develop stories based on student interests, current events, school happenings, or even in nonsense stories such as "Mad-Libs." This creates interest and helps the words come alive for your students.

134. Use manipulatives and active games to teach vocabulary.

Underachievers are particularly motivated by games and other hands-on activities. Learning vocabulary lends itself well to all types of games, such as Bingo, Pick Two, Vocabulary Jeopardy and Scrabble to vocabulary bees and team relay races using vocabulary words. Games are a great strategy for teaching vocabulary in any content area.

135. Use mapping techniques or diagrams to visually show concepts or vocabulary.

These techniques are particularly effective with visual learners who remember and understand better when they can see a picture of the word or concept.

Inspiration® and Kidspiration® software is an excellent resource to use when teaching students mapping techniques. It allows students to think in either graphic or text mode, creates mind maps for students and links ideas. This is a wonderful tool for teaching content vocabulary because it shows students links between similar words, meanings and concepts.

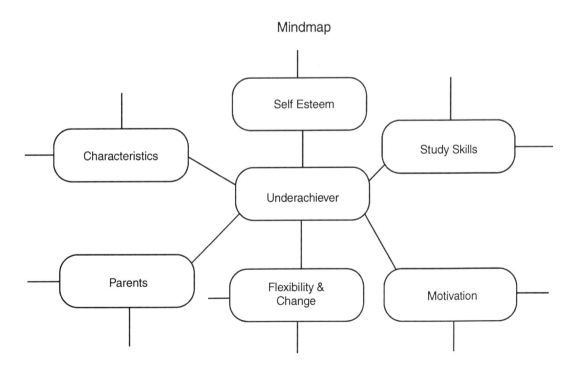

Chapter 4

MOTIVATION - AN ESSENTIAL ELEMENT OF ACHIEVEMENT

"School is boring," announced twelve-year-old Brian.

"Yeah," agreed Teresa. *"I usually think of some reason to get out of class. The work is just too stupid. I hate answering all of those questions from the social studies book."*

"My teacher says all I do is daydream," chimed in Katonia. *"But if I think about what I can do at the mall when I get out of school, the time goes faster."*

"I sleep in class," declared Chris as he sat slouched in his chair with his arms folded and with a smirk on his face. *"I just tell 'ol Mrs. Moore that I won't do the work, and I don't!"*

These four middle school students sat in my office discussing some of their problems in school. All four were identified as high ability students, yet all four were chronic underachievers who found little relevance in school activities. Their teachers had described them in the following ways:

Refuses to do assignments
Sleeps in class
Openly defiant
Negative body language
Poor attendance
Needs to leave class often
Spends time daydreaming
Has excuses for incomplete work

All four of these students lacked an essential element needed for achievement:
MOTIVATION.

MOTIVATION
WHAT IS IT?

Motivation is the drive and desire for success in some endeavor. It requires initiative, interest and dedication in focusing on and working toward a goal. Motivation involves a sense of purpose, a feeling of enthusiasm and an ability to have self direction. All of us are motivated to do something. In the school setting, we want that something to involve academic goals, high standards of excellence, and an attitude that says learning is important. Without motivation, teaching is for naught. Yet, sadly, a lack of motivation in school is a characteristic of most underachievers.

DESTROYERS OF MOTIVATION

No Expectation of Success

Motivation and success go hand-in-hand. Success breeds motivation and motivation brings success. In fact, before any student is willing to learn, he or she must believe that he or she will succeed.

Without this belief, the student will not even be motivated to try and the whole process of teaching and learning will break down before it is ever begun. Students who have a history of failure in school have difficulty developing any expectations for success. Therefore, when test scores and/or report card grades are used as the only source of success, and there are no meaningful rewards for effort, motivation quickly wanes in these students. When students have no expectation of success, motivation is destroyed.

Fear of Failure

A lack of motivation is tied directly to a student's low self esteem and poor self concept. A history of failure in academic or social areas in school can be responsible for this, as can the anxiety created by real or perceived threats of failure. Often an unmotivated student's perception is that his or her efforts will result in failure, rejection, or judgmental attitudes on the part of teachers, parents, or peers. Such a student decides, consciously or unconsciously, that not trying at all is a better choice than facing possible failure and rejection. From this point of view, the failure somehow looks better if he or she wasn't trying in the first place.

Unmotivated students often feel alienated from their peers and teachers. This happens because they feel criticized, ridiculed or socially inadequate and feel they are accepted only if they compare favorably with their peers and/or siblings.

Motivation is of major concern to teachers who are trying to work with underachievers. Without motivation, it is almost impossible to reverse underachievement.

DEVELOPING MOTIVATIONAL STRATEGIES

There are a number of common elements found in all motivational strategies. First, educators need to genuinely respect and accept each student. An understanding of the individual child, his or her background and interests, and how to develop each child's self concept are important considerations when developing motivational strategies.

The classroom climate is also important. A motivating teacher is flexible and energetic and uses a variety of teaching techniques. He or she is positive, caring and inviting. The strategies in this chapter suggest ways to motivate underachievers.

Successful Strategies . . .

Have a Motivational Teaching Style

136. Use attention-attracting materials to capture your student's curiosity and interest.

Classroom materials, including books, manipulatives, bulletin boards and displays should be colorful, interesting and varied. When your students walk into your classroom, their attention should immediately be captured by the environment. For example, one classroom I visited recently captured my attention immediately. The class had been studying Japan. Japanese paper fish hung from the ceiling, pictures of Japan covered the walls, each student's name was displayed on a card written in Japanese, and a hands-on learning center with Japanese artifacts was in one corner of the room. These attention-attracting materials served as a wonderful motivator for the students.

137. Use riddles, jokes, humorous stories or anecdotes as attention-getters in your lessons.

We live in an age of nonstop pop culture. Our students are accustomed to a barrage of humorous (and sometimes off-color) verbal one-liners from their favorite television performers, sports heroes and movie stars. While a teacher should not need to compete with a comedian, it helps in motivating students when interest-catching riddles, jokes or stories are told during the lesson. Teachers should learn how to be good storytellers who can use humor to make a point or introduce a topic. If you have no natural talent for this, find books of riddles or logic puzzles and challenge your students to solve one at the beginning of each day.

138. Give students time to think over the question before answering.

Many teachers are so anxious to cover the material or go on with the lesson that they forget to give students time to actually think! Students who are not sure of the answer will be more motivated if they know you will give them time before answering and that you won't call on someone else or answer it yourself. Waiting for student answers also gives underachievers the message that their input is important and that they can't always count on someone else to do the thinking and have the answer.

139. Make the objectives of the assignment explicit, showing practical value in the assignment and its relationship to other kinds of knowledge and skills.

The complaint heard most often from underachievers is that school is boring and that there is no reason to learn what is being taught. Make sure that you know why you are giving each assignment and that there is value in asking your students to do the task you have assigned. Avoid needless "busy work." This seems to be one of the greatest destroyers of motivation for underachieving students.

140. Personalize the topic.

Involve your students on a personal level with the topic at hand. Relate the assignment to past experiences that your class has shared together or to experiences you are aware that your students have had individually. When you teach math word problems, rewrite the textbook version so that they are personalized to fit the names and experiences of your students. Take the time to get to know your underachievers personally. The better you know them, the more successful you will be with this strategy.

141. Videotape your own classroom in order to observe your teaching techniques and/or the behavior of your underachievers.

We rarely have the luxury of seeing ourselves as others see us. One way to accomplish this is to set up a video camera in the back of your classroom and let it run unnoticed for two or three hours. You will discover many things about your own teaching style and about the interaction that occurs between you and your students. No one else needs to see this video, so this is a non- threatening way to do serious self-evaluation.

A variation of this strategy is to ask another teacher to observe your teaching style or to observe the behaviors of a particular student. This can give you valuable feedback from a peer's perspective.

142. Include demonstrations and simulations as part of your lessons.

"A picture is worth a thousand words," as the old saying goes. And so it is for our students. Demonstrations and simulations provide the real-life picture for students and bring concrete meaning to abstract concepts. Role-playing simulations and computer simulations are both excellent ways to use this strategy.

143. Plan activities where students perform skits and/or use costumes.

Another real-life picture can be brought to students through the dramatic arts. Performing skits related to classroom activities has a high interest level and is very motivating for most students. Particularly motivational are skits which are tied to television shows, movies or popular music. If you don't have the time for elaborate skits, try readers' theater where students read from a script without memorizing it. The motivational impact will be much the same.

144. Involve your students in food activities which relate to the topic being taught.

It is the rare student indeed who is not motivated by food! Instead of using food as a reward or extrinsic motivator as is commonly done, include food in your lesson plans when it is appropriate to the lesson. Social studies lessons often lend themselves to learning about the food in a particular geographic region. Math concepts can be demonstrated by the use of food, as can some lessons in science and health.

145. Plan for your students to do work on the chalkboard or dry erase board.

Allow your students to demonstrate their skills or work through problems on the chalkboard. Perhaps it is the kinesthetic appeal of chalk or markers combined with being able to get up out of one's seat. For whatever reason, most students are motivated by being able to use the board as long as they do not have to lose face in front of the class by showing they do not know something that everyone else knows.

146. Give your students their own individual dry erase board and an erasable marker to use at their seats.

Individual dry erase boards can be made from a large piece of bathroom wallboard you can get at almost any home improvement or supply store. If you tell them you are a teacher, these businesses will usually cut the dry erase boards to your specifications at no cost. 12"x12" is usually a good size for each dry erase board. Students can figure out math problems, write spelling or vocabulary words, or answer a question you have asked by writing on the dry erase boards then holding up their answers for you to see. This strategy almost always results in high student involvement and motivation.

Provide Opportunities for the Exploration of Interest Areas

147. Find out what your underachieving students' areas of interest are.

Learn about the out-of-school interests of your students. Most students have a "passion area" of interest which can be a source of inner motivation. Try to discover the "passion areas" of your underachievers and build on these in the classroom. Interest inventories, informal conversation, parent conferences, journals and written assignments where the student chooses the topic are all sources from which to identify the students' interest areas.

148. Give assignments that build on strengths and interests.

Develop units of content that are connected to the interests of your students. These can be individual interests or a topic of interest to the whole class. Pay particular attention to the interests and strengths of your underachieving students. Make sure to show your students how the assignment is relevant to their interests.

149. Assign independent study projects.

Independent study projects are most successful with underachievers when you give students a wide range of flexible choices. Give your students a choice of topics, a choice of projects or products, and a choice of how to assess and determine a grade. Projects tend to be of higher quality when they are presented to a wide audience.

See Encouraging Achievement by Carolyn Coil (Pieces of Learning, publisher) and Autonomous Learner Model: Optimizing Ability by George Betts and Jolene Kercher (ALPS Publishing) for suggestions about how to structure independent study.

150. Allow students to become "Resident Experts" in topics of particular interest.

Some underachievers know a great deal about topics of extreme interest to them. Allow them to continue studying their own special topics in depth and acknowledge them as the school's "Resident Experts." This not only boosts self confidence, but it also enhances research skills and study skills. Create a database of topics and student Resident Experts to distribute to every teacher in the school. These students can become valuable resources to teachers and can do Resident Expert presentations for other classes. Because most underachievers need structure even when studying a topic of interest, use the **Resident Expert Planning Form** on the next page to help each student plan his or her research.

RESIDENT EXPERT PLANNING FORM

Name: _____

Topic: _____

<u>Things I already know about this topic: (Use other side of paper if needed)</u>

<u>What I want to learn about this topic:</u>

<u>Resources I could use:</u>

<u>My learning plan with checkpoint dates:</u>

	<u>Activity</u>	<u>Checkpoint date</u>
1.	_____	_____
2.	_____	_____
3.	_____	_____
4.	_____	_____

Reproducible form for student use.

151. Contact outside experts in your students' interest or passion areas and ask them to evaluate your students' final projects.

One choice in project evaluation (see Strategy 149) is to invite experts from your community to evaluate your student projects. Explore school/business partnerships to examine the feasibility of people from the business community working with your students. This lends validity to the assessment process and is often a motivator to students. This process of evaluation is especially motivating to an underachiever who is able to talk to an adult who is an expert in his or her interest area. Sometimes this can be the beginning of a mentoring relationship (see Strategy 152).

152. Assist your underachieving students in finding a mentor.

A mentor/student partnership is a special relationship that takes work and commitment on the part of both persons involved. In order for a mentoring relationship to be successful, the mentor must agree to work with the student at regular intervals throughout the year. The student must be open to the idea of working with a mentor, and there must be a congenial blend of personalities. When these elements are in place, a mentor can be invaluable to the underachieving student. Explore sources for finding mentors in your community. Some school districts have a mentor resource list while in other districts you will have to search for resources on your own. If the right mentor is found, this strategy can work wonders with underachievers.

153. Use February 2 (Groundhog Day) as "Job Shadow Day."

Motivate your underachievers and make their classwork seem more relevant by participating in National Groundhog Job Shadow Day. The goal of this day is to demonstrate to students the connection between school, their interests and careers. A national organization promotes February 2 as a day for job shadowing to introduce students to the requirements of a job or profession. It also encourages an ongoing relationship between the student and the adult he or she is shadowing. For more information visit www.jobshadow.org

154. Spend time working with your underachiever one-on-one.

It is difficult with today's hectic school schedules to find time to be with individual students one-on-one. However, if you can schedule such times, they are invaluable in providing underachievers the special attention they need, not just for motivation, but also to build self esteem and improve study skills. Perhaps you can find time within your classroom schedule for these individualized meetings. If not, try to arrange some out-of-class time to give your underachievers personal attention. In this time together, ask the student to explain his frustration with school, a particular class, or an assignment. Opening up does not happen all at once, but your attempt to show personal attention usually will pay off in gains made in student motivation.

155. Have a "Four Day Work Week" with earned special activities on Fridays.

Time management experts say most of us do 80% of our work in 20% of our time. They also tell us that work expands to take up whatever time has been allotted for it. These two axioms of time management can be applied to our students as well as to adults. An incentive to finish the required schoolwork in four days rather than five is motivational to students who know that special activities await them on Fridays if the work is finished. Underachievers work well under this type of time pressure if they are motivated by the reward.

156. Institute a "Friday Question Day."

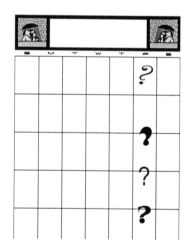

Some underachievers love to pose "off the wall" questions, partly because they like to get the teacher distracted from the topic for the day and partly because they like divergent and creative thinking. If you have questioners who constantly distract you and the class from the task at hand, try instituting Friday Question Day. All week, the would-be questioners write down their questions as the lesson is going on. They can post their questions on the board or on chart paper at the end of each class. On Friday, the entire class deals with the questions that are posted and decides the best strategies for answering them or discussing them.

157. Allow for alternative products that require less pencil/paper activities and more hands-on activities.

Many underachievers are kinesthetic learners who learn by using their hands, manipulating objects, and moving around the room. They are least adept at sitting quietly in a desk doing work with paper and pencil. In general, schools are not structured for such learners. Structure your classroom to allow for hands-on activities to meet the needs of these students.

158. Allow your students to test out of routine work.

Underachievers, like most other students, dislike drill and practice assignments particularly when they already know the skill involved. While achievers will do routine assignments in order to keep up their grades, underachievers resist and refuse to do the work. Motivation falls and they turn off to school. To avoid this scenario, give pretests to establish the skill level of your students and require that they practice only those skills in which they are deficient. (See Curriculum Compacting, Strategy 116).

159. Give opportunities for individualized choices.

Design a flexible program which gives students choices in as many areas as possible. Independent study projects (see Strategy 149) are just one example. Another possibility is to develop a contract with each student that gives a number of choices and options. For samples of learning contracts and student choice activities, see Teaching Tools for the 21st Century by Carolyn Coil, Pieces of Learning, publisher and Teaching Gifted Kids in the Regular Classroom by Susan Winebrenner, Free Spirit Publishing.

160. Have activity days as an incentive for students who have completed all of their assignments with a 'C' grade or better.

An extrinsic motivator, activity days are usually planned at the end of a set interval of time. Some suggested activities are: chess, music, field trips, guest speakers, computer time, creative dramatics, sharing hobbies or interests, logic games, non-traditional activities for academics, and other intellectually challenging activities.

161. Minimize the use of worksheets.

Student worksheets, while useful and appropriate on occasion, are generally not very motivational for students. One approach to get away from the use of these reproducible student handouts is to declare one day of each week a school-wide "no worksheets." Encourage all teachers to do hands-on activities involving critical and creative thinking on that day.

162. Allow students flexibility in turning in assignments as long as they are turned in by a given date.

This strategy works well for some underachievers and is a disaster for others, so use it with care. Some underachieving students work well with less structure and flexible assignments. When they think they have some choices they produce more, they become more self motivated and their achievement improves. Other underachievers need the structure imposed by teachers and parents. These students will procrastinate and achieve even less if flexible due dates are established for assignments. Know your students well before using this strategy; it will be very successful with some.

163. Use impromptu speeches as ways to motivate your students and increase interest in classroom activities.

For a chance of pace, use the last five or ten minutes of the day or class period for impromptu speeches. This activity will improve your students' speaking and listening skills and increase interest, especially at the end of the day. Read from a book of quotes or thoughts for the day and call on a student to give an impromptu two minute speech on the topic. This short talk should have an introduction, several thoughts or arguments to back up the student's point of view and a conclusion. Call on one or two students daily. Over time, most students will look forward to this activity and the oral communication skills of all your students will improve. An excellent source for quotes is www.creativequotations.com which cites quotations from at least three different people on the date of their birth.

164. Give opportunities for student involvement in planning and evaluating classroom activities.

Classroom activities are more motivating for students when they are involved in planning the activities and then in evaluating the effectiveness of those activities they have planned. While this process is time consuming, it is very beneficial in terms of teaching students planning, decision making, and consensus building skills and in creating a feeling of interest in and ownership of classroom activities. If you use this strategy, make sure that your underachievers are actively involved in the planning process. If a group of highly achieving students takes over the leadership, the underachievers will feel no commitment to what has been planned.

165. Assess students' learning styles and modalities.

There are a number of assessment instruments that measure ways students learn. Students are always interested in learning more about themselves. An understanding of their own learning styles/modalities and your teaching style will help them understand what type of teaching they respond to best. In assessing the ways individual students learn best, you may also be able to adjust assignment choices to better fit your underachievers. Use the two checklists on the next three pages for a quick assessment of learning styles and learning modalities. The first checklist refers to the work of Dr. Anthony Gregorc. For more information on this topic and to see how to plan lessons based on learning styles and modalities see <u>Teaching Tools for the 21st Century</u> by Carolyn Coil, Pieces of Learning, publisher.

Concrete sequential students like to:

_____ Read or listen to, and then follow directions.
_____ Take notes, look at charts or diagrams, and do outlines.
_____ Participate in structured learning, including pencil and paper exercises.
_____ Have an organized teacher.
_____ Know what the marking system is and what the teacher's specific expectations.

Abstract sequential students like to:

_____ Read different kinds of books, usually from beginning to end sequentially.
_____ Listen to audio tapes, compact disks and lectures, see videos, films and slides, and work on the computer and other electronic learning tools.
_____ Help other students understand the subject matter or what they've read.
_____ Find THE answer to a problem, but are uncomfortable with multiple answers and possibilities.
_____ Look at things logically, even situations where a logical solution is not necessarily the best one or does not solve the problem.

Concrete random students like to:

_____ Complete a product or project for a classroom assignment.
_____ Brainstorm creative ideas.
_____ Take risks. Concrete random students will volunteer for anything!
_____ Do things by trial and error.
_____ Solve problems alone.
_____ Avoid IQ and achievement tests.

Abstract random students like to:

_____ Listen to, learn from, and respond to their classmates.
_____ Work in groups and will become the natural leaders in small groups.
_____ Do short reading assignments and often do not read books sequentially.
_____ Use emotions and intuition.
_____ Have lots of things going on at once.

Reproducible for student use.

LEARNING MODALITIES CHECKLIST

Check items in each category that describe an individual student. The strongest learning modality or modalities will be those with the most items checked.

Student Name _____

Visual learners

- ❑ Are good with detail
- ❑ Learn by seeing, watching demonstrations
- ❑ Often remember whatever they have written down
- ❑ Can recall the placement of words and pictures on a page
- ❑ Like descriptive reading
- ❑ Enjoy and learn from visual displays and colors
- ❑ Recognize words by sight and people by face rather than name
- ❑ Have a vivid imagination and think in pictures
- ❑ Are deliberate problem solvers and plan solutions in advance
- ❑ Facial expressions are a good indication of their emotions

Auditory/Verbal learners

- ❑ Enjoy listening but are always ready to talk
- ❑ Like music, rap, poetry, rhyming words
- ❑ Enjoy dialogues, skits and debates
- ❑ Have auditory word attack skills and learn words phonetically
- ❑ Talk to themselves, repeating information aloud
- ❑ Are distracted by sounds
- ❑ Talk out problems and the pros and cons of a situation
- ❑ Express emotion through changes in pitch, tone and volume of voice
- ❑ Are not detail persons; tend to be global thinkers
- ❑ Learn through verbal instructions from others or themselves

Kinesthetic/Tactile learners

❑ Learn by hands-on experiences

❑ Prefer direct involvement rather than being a spectator

❑ Enjoy the performing arts and/or athletics

❑ Like working with materials, machinery and tools

❑ Prefer action/adventure stories and videos

❑ Communicate feelings through body language

❑ Experiment with ideas to see how they will work in the real world

❑ Touch, feel, manipulate, and play with objects

❑ Show emotions physically by jumping, hugging, applauding, etc.

❑ Remember what they have done rather than what they have seen or read

Technological learners

❑ Are mechanically oriented

❑ Know how to use technological tools without formal instruction

❑ Enjoy using a video camera

❑ Obtain much of their information electronically

❑ Like integrated learning activities

❑ Would like to learn everything via the computer

❑ Spend much of their spare time on the computer or playing video games

❑ Know how to work with and use new software and hardware

❑ Interact and communicate with others via the Internet

❑ Understand how to integrate various technologies

Reproducible for student use.

...to your

st underachievers.
drill and practice
derachievers who
need remediation
(see Strategy 117). Technology is also excellent for developing critical and creative
thinking (see Strategy 168), research, communication beyond the classroom, and as a
way to access instruction that would not be
available otherwise. Ways to use technology
with students are unlimited! Don't limit its use just as a reward to your achievers.
Use it as a motivator and a learning tool for your underachievers.

167. Use word processing as a tool for improving writing skills.

Allow your students to use word processors whenever possible when they are doing
essays or reports. This works especially well because underachievers often do not like
to do written work but they do like to use the computer. Word processing can reduce
frustrations with poor handwriting, grammar and spelling. Editing and revising written work is quicker, and the finished product usually looks great. All of these factors
are important motivators for underachievers.

168. Teach problem solving and critical thinking using Webquests.

Webquests were first developed by Bernie Dodge of San Diego State University in
1995. They encourage students to use the information they gather from the Internet
to solve a problem. Webquests are inquiry based and encourage analysis, synthesis
and evaluation. You can create your own Webquests or can use Webquests created
by others. For more information and for sample Webquests, see internet site:
http://edweb.sdsu.edu/webquest

169. Use simulations to teach both basic and higher level thinking skills.

Simulations are highly motivational because they involve active thinking and real
life problem solving. Computer simulations can focus students on real life situations
or situations which may have existed in the past or which may exist in the future.
There are a number of excellent commercially developed simulations as well as a

multitude on the Internet. Webquests (see Strategy 168) are often simulations. Be sure to be familiar with any simulation yourself before introducing it to your students. This strategy is almost guaranteed to motivate all of your students, including your underachievers!

170. Show your students how to use the Internet for research.

The Internet contains a wealth of information about almost any conceivable subject. Underachievers, like almost all other students, love to 'Surf the Net.' Aimless surfing, however, does not lend itself to developing appropriate research skills. Underachievers need structure in their learning, especially when doing independent work. Develop guidelines for using the Internet and teach these along with other research skills. Guidelines for reliable print, e-mail and web sources can be found in Encouraging Achievement by Carolyn Coil, Pieces of Learning, publisher. Online check http://discoveryschool.com/schrockguide/ Kathy Schrock's Guide for Educators.

171. Encourage multimedia student products.

Producing a multimedia project is an especially motivating and high interest task. Hands-on use of HyperStudio®, PowerPoint®, Inspiration® and other integrated software packages along with digitizing images, video and audio production, animation, etc. is an excellent motivator for many underachievers, especially for underachievers who are turned off by routine schoolwork and who already know essential skills in reading, writing and math.

172. Assess students using electronic portfolios.

Electronic portfolios can show what students know in traditional ways and also in solving authentic problems and in using telecommunications. A collection of student work in the Information Age seems much more real and therefore more motivational to students when it includes new technologies as well as paper and pencil activities.

173. Build your own web site.

This is a terrific strategy for communicating with your students, their parents and the community at large. It's one way to relate what's happening in your classroom and your school, post a class newsletter, showcase student work, give information about upcoming events and homework assignments, and provide links to other relevant sites on the web. This helps underachievers and their parents keep up with homework assignments and may motivate some underachievers to produce work worthy of being displayed on the web site. A free easy-to-use program for creating your own web site is myschoolonline.com. This resource can be obtained through the Family Education Network, 20 Park Plaza, Suite 1420, Boston, MA 02116. Toll-free phone: 1-800-498-3264.

174. Investigate ways to use telecommunications, video conferencing and other new technologies in your school or classroom

Continual new developments and changes in technology may make the above list of strategies almost obsolete before this book is published! Continue to investigate new technologies and ask how they can be used to benefit your students, particularly your underachievers. Virtual field trips, connecting classrooms and campuses for special lectures and assemblies, video seminars between students in different locations, special interest mini-classes and practicing foreign languages with native speakers around the globe are just a few of the many uses you will find for technology.

175. Show underachievers connections between school and the "real world" through e-mail interviews.

Ask them to search the Internet to learn about a particular career field or profession which is related to the content being studied in your class. Have them find web sites with e-mail addresses and interview professionals via e-mail, asking particularly about the connections between school and the world of work. A set of sample e-mail interview questions is below.

An E-Mail Interview with a Professional

1. What is your job title?

2. How long have you been in this particular job?

3. Which subjects or courses that you took in school have helped you the most in your job?

4. How is my study of _____ connected with what you do in your job or profession?

5. What is the best thing about your job? What's the worst thing?

6. If you could do it over, what things would you change about your school years?

7. What advice can you give to me and other students in ___ grade if we want to go into your career field?

8. What do you think is the most useful thing I will study in school?

---

176. Increase the underachieving student's level of perceived competence.

One's perception of his or her competence to do a given task increases the motivation to do the task. On the other hand, a low level of perceived competence decreases motivation. Encourage your underachievers, indicating your assurances that they are able to do what is required. Your belief in their ability to be successful will help it to happen!

177. Show the student the similarities between the task at hand and other tasks at which he or she has succeeded in the past.

In working to increase the level of perceived competence your underachievers have (see Strategy 176) point out the successes they have had in the past. Emphasize the ways in which the task at hand is similar to things they have already done successfully.

178. Design an honor roll that recognizes progress toward a goal and a student's "Personal Best," not just As and Bs.

This provides the student with a sense of progress and focuses on growth the student makes, not on how far behind he or she is compared with other students. In such a system, the student is competing with himself or herself, not with other students. Athletic competition where an athlete attempts to beat his or her own best record in progress toward a goal is similar to this idea, as are the steps of progress from white belt to black belt in the martial arts. A variation on this strategy is to have a class Honor Roll which honors students who have completed a certain amount of work.

179. Make sure the student can see an end to the assignment.

Achievement is easier to strive toward when one can see the "light at the end of the tunnel." Assignments that appear to last forever with no end and no reward in sight are particularly difficult for underachievers. If an assignment seems too long, structure it so that it becomes several shorter tasks.

180. Be sure your directions are clear.

When you give an assignment, make sure you know exactly what your expectations are for completion and how you want the assignment to be done. Then, give clear directions so that your students also know what is expected. Achievers will tackle a task or assignment without clear direction, but underachievers often use a lack of direction as an excuse for not getting the assignment done.

181. Make sure the assignment is not beyond the student's ability level.

There is nothing more frustrating than to attempt to do something that is so far above one's ability level that failure is assured. When an underachiever faces such an assignment and sees no chance of success, he gives up before he ever begins. Examine your assignments carefully to ensure the possibility of success for all of your students.

182. Have a classroom contest where you control the difficulty and type of questions given to each student or student team.

When you control which questions are given to which students, you can make sure some of the questions given to your underachievers are ones which will bring them success. Success builds on itself and increases both motivation and self esteem.

Develop Creativity to Increase Motivation

183. Provide opportunities for creative development.

It's important to find ways to encourage children to develop creative skills, talents, and abilities. Don't spend all of your class time preparing students for competency and achievement tests. Creative thinking is often lost when you do this. When a child sees that he can create something successfully, it builds his competency, skill and self confidence in all areas.

184. Develop a variety of creative ways to present book reports.

If your curriculum includes book reports, be flexible in your requirements as to how the reports may be given. When all students are required to read a book, a number of different ways to give the report should be acceptable. Brainstorm possibilities for original book reports with your students. You will be surprised at some of their creative ideas.

185. Use a 'pizza box portfolio' for a writing portfolio.

Get donations of unused large pizza boxes from a local pizza restaurant. Give one to each student to take home and decorate in a creative way. Some may paint their boxes while others may make a collage or cover it with photos. Over the year the students store their best writing in their pizza box portfolios. Take a day each month for students to choose which pieces of writing will go in the portfolio and to complete a self evaluation. Underachievers are motivated by the hands-on aspect of the initial project, by the creativity involved, and by the choices and self evaluation inherent in making this type of portfolio.

186. Make sure that some of your classroom activities require divergent thinking.

Many underachievers are excellent divergent thinkers, but they rarely have the opportunity to use this skill in the school setting. Use creative problem solving, brainstorming, questioning techniques which involve active learning, and simulation activities to develop divergent thinking skills.

Several excellent resources for questioning skills and divergent thinking include Questioning Makes the Difference, Thinking is the Key, Active Questioning, and Quick Question Workbook by Nancy L. Johnson, Pieces of Learning, publisher.

187. Evaluate your lessons for motivation and creative thinking.

Most teachers want to facilitate creative thinking in their classrooms, but this focus is often lost because more concentration is placed on meeting the goals and objectives for specific subject areas. Use the self-evaluation form on the next page to help you evaluate the opportunities for creative thinking provided in your classroom.

Make several copies of the form and put them in a notebook, file folder or other convenient place. When you have a motivating or creative lesson, take a few moments to reflect on what you've done and fill out one of the forms. Over time you will have a collection of creative and motivational strategies and ideas that work especially well for you. This is also great documentation for your teaching portfolio.

In addition to self-evaluation, you may want to use this form as a springboard to sharing ideas with other teachers. At a grade level or department meeting, ask everyone to take a few minutes to think about a creative or motivating lesson they have done. Then have each person fill out a form. This provides a structure for sharing great ideas or for brainstorming the elements of successful motivating lessons.

EVALUATING CLASSROOM ACTIVITIES
FOR CREATIVITY AND MOTIVATION

1. What portions of the lesson produced a positive attitude in my students?

2. What interests of my students provided the focus for this activity?

3. What evidence do I have that this activity helped create a positive classroom climate for my students?

4. In what ways did my students feel successful after doing this activity?

5. How was divergent thinking used in the lesson?

6. What were the most creative parts of this activity?

7. What did my students enjoy the most?

8. Which parts of the lesson did my students find boring?

9. Which elements in this activity could be adapted to motivate students when I plan other lessons?

10. What would I change if I did the same lesson again?

Extrinsic and Intrinsic Motivators

When teachers hear the word "motivation," the first thing that comes to mind often is an extrinsic reward. Extrinsic motivators certainly play a part in motivation. Most of us probably would not go to work every day without the extrinsic motivator called the pay-check!

External motivators also play a part in student motivation. However, smiley faces, stickers, and the like work only for a short time because they soon lose their reward value. Good grades and the feeling of success associated with them motivate students when they are linked to long term goals or if the students are people pleasers. Extrinsic motivators work if they are desired by the student in and of themselves. For example, earning tickets to a ball game or being able to go on a major field trip have been cited as successful motivators by teachers I have worked with.

Effective motivators over the long term are generally more intrinsic in nature. Giving the student a sense of personal autonomy and control over his or her successes and failures is a powerful motivator. Positive verbal and nonverbal reinforcement motivates as does the opportunity to participate in interesting, challenging activities. The student's ability to develop positive relationships with people who care results in the most effective long term motivation.

Use extrinsic motivators when they work for you, but use them with a long term view in mind. They are the building blocks to the intrinsic motivation found in an achieving, independent, self-motivated learner!

Chapter 5

WORKING WITH PARENTS OF UNDERACHIEVERS

> *"I hate to see a child with so much potential do so little,"* remarked Mr. Bowen, a fifth grade teacher. *"I think the main problem comes from the home. Tom's parents have high expectations but they're not firm or consistent in what is allowed at home on a day-to-day basis. I think they are unsure of themselves as parents and are anxious about what they should be expecting academically and emotionally from Tom. He takes advantage of the situation and manipulates them. He seems to have more power and responsibility at home than he has the maturity or judgment to use. The parents need some guidance. As a teacher, I can't solve the underachievement problem alone!"*

Parents of underachievers play an important role in working toward solutions to the problem of underachievement. A multitude of factors come into consideration when working with these parents.

Some parents exhibit high levels of anxiety when dealing with their children. They are not firm or consistent in setting expectations and standards, and they may exhibit negative attitudes toward their children or toward the school system. Their children may become underachievers because they, in turn, internalize the parents' negative attitudes. Conversely, other parents overly identify with their children and put too much pressure on them to do well in school. In this case, the children rebel and do much less than they are capable of doing.

The causes of underachievement are varied and complex, but usually are a combination of factors present at home and at school. Establishing a good working relationship with the parents of your underachieving students is extremely helpful in working through this problem.

Successful Strategies . . .

Know the Family Background

188. Be familiar with the child's background.

One of the first steps in understanding underachievers is to know something about the family background. Sometimes the major causes of underachievement are found in the home; but this is not true in all cases. Knowing the particular problems and circumstances in the home situation is essential in dealing with underachievement problems.

189. Be sensitive to clues about what is going on at home.

In general, we have our students with us in school six or seven hours a day. The remainder of their time is spent in their neighborhoods and home situations. Many families are in crisis. Problems of abuse, neglect, poverty and violence are everyday occurrences in some homes. Some parents are too busy with their own professional lives to pay much attention to their children. In other cases, children move from one home to another with little or no stability. All of these problems have direct impact upon our students. Be sensitive to the situations your underachievers face at home.

190. Initiate intervention through community agencies if it is needed.

Educators are very much aware of the problems mentioned above (see Strategy 189). Most of these problems are beyond our ability and authority to deal with at school. Be knowledgeable of community agencies and other organizations that work with children and their families. As an educator, you can be a valuable resource if you know where to look for help.

191. Begin a weekend school for both students and parents.

This strategy works particularly well in language minority communities where the parents are struggling to learn English and where programs promote bilingual family literacy. Reading instruction in the native language develops skills that help in the acquisition of English and general academic skills. Underachievers sometimes blossom when they have a chance to take the leadership in a learning environment involving their parents as well as themselves.

Initiate Positive Communication with Parents

192. Mail, fax or e-mail positive notes/letters to parents regularly.

Parents of underachievers rarely receive positive notes from school, so this will be a welcome change. Make sure your note emphasizes something good about their children. You may want to keep a file of preprinted notes. Plan to send home a specific number each week, with special emphasis on finding something positive to say to the parents of your underachievers.

193. Schedule regular communication with parents.

All teachers are busy people! Most teachers have good intentions when it comes to communicating with parents. However, other priorities take precedence and the communication does not occur unless there is a problem or emergency. The operative word in this strategy is 'schedule.' The communication won't happen unless you schedule and plan for it.

194. Make positive phone calls.

One of the most effective techniques in parent/teacher communication is a positive phone call. Do this early in the year before there are any problems with students. A brief update is all that is needed. To your advantage, if you establish a habit of positive phone calls, the lines of communication will be open if and when there is a problem. Continue positive phone calls throughout the school year. Keep a record of who you called, what you discussed and the parents' reactions or concerns.

195. Make a quick response to any parent communication.

A good guideline is to respond in less than 24 hours. If a parent is contacting you, it is likely that he or she is having a problem or concern about the child. Your quick response will alleviate parent anxiety and deal with the problem or concern before it escalates.

196. Make home visits to parents when appropriate.

Seeing your students' home environments provides invaluable insight for the classroom teacher. As a practical matter, it is probably impossible to visit the home of every student you teach. Target your underachievers for special attention. Explore the feasibility of visiting their homes. This home/school connection could be extremely beneficial as you work on ways to solve the underachievement problem.

197. Send home regular progress reports.

Some school districts require this; it's an important strategy to use with under-achievers whether it is required or not. Updating parents regularly, especially when students are not achieving, avoids surprises and anger at report card time. Additionally, underachievement is easier to reverse when it is caught and dealt with early.

198. Get business cards for yourself.

Having a business card identifies you as a professional and gives the message that you are available for consultation and problem solving. Make sure your card has pertinent information - your name, school name, address, phone, fax, e-mail and web site. Don't include your home phone number unless you don't mind being called at home. Parents of underachievers are often grateful to have a teacher who is willing to listen and give them suggestions.

199. Use new technologies to communicate with parents.

As new technologies become available in your school or school district, ask yourself how these could enhance communication with parents. Homework hotlines, video conferencing, voice mail, e-mail, web sites and video portfolios are some examples. There are many more, and new technologies appear almost daily.

Parent/Teacher Conferences and Meetings

200. Recognize that home and school must work together to build a child's positive self-image.

School and home together build up or break down a child's self image. Parents and teachers must work as partners in building self-esteem in children. (See Strategies 4, 5, 6 and 11.)

201. Include the student in the parent/teacher conference when possible and appropriate.

When you have a conference with the parent of an underachiever, it is beneficial to include the student as well. Problems that are discussed with the student present are more likely to be acted upon when the student has input into the proposed solutions. In such a conference, talk openly about problems the student has. Then make some decisions along with the student concerning actions to take to help solve the problems and concerns that have been identified.

202. Hold parent meetings at convenient times for parents.

A problem in working with parent groups is trying to find a time when parents are willing and able to come to meetings. The pace and busyness of modern life make this a difficult problem to solve. Each community and each group of parents has a best time for them. Try several options for meeting days and times to see what works best for your parent group.

203. Help to organize a parent support group for parents of underachievers.

Parents don't realize that there are other parents who have similar problems with their underachievers. Parents can help one another and support one another as they deal with the problems that underachievers have. In one parent support group, a typical comment was: "I had that happen last year and this is what I did . . . " As a teacher, you do not need to take the responsibility of running the support group, but you may need to provide the impetus and organization to bring these parents together so they know one another.

204. Provide parent training and offer incentives for parents of underachievers to come.

Parents of underachievers can benefit from specific training in how to work with their children. The most effective training is done in partnership with the teacher. Plan to have training focused on how to deal with underachieving students. Target the parents of your underachievers and personally invite them to come. Offer to pick them up and take them to the training session as your guests. Provide babysitting as needed. This personal attention will not only insure their attendance, but may be a catalyst in creating a home/school partnership with them.

Parents and Schoolwork

205. Facilitate written communication between underachieving students and their parents regarding their schoolwork.

Suggestions for implementing this strategy:
- Have students keep a daily school journal that goes back and forth between home and school.
- Send student work home each week in a special envelope for parents. Request a parent signature.
- Send home a weekly newsletter written especially for parents.
- Post assignments on your web site (see Strategy 173) or voice mail.

206. Have a written homework policy.

Develop a written homework policy that states the expectations of students, parents and the teacher. Make sure parents are informed about classwork, upcoming tests and projects, and ways they can help their child to study.

207. Begin a parent-teacher homework hotline.

Establish hours when parents may call you in the evening to ask questions about homework. Send homework update slips informing parents of an important test or a long range project well in advance of the date it is due. Encourage parents to make sure their child uses a home checklist of supplies (see Strategy 57). Ask parents to sign completed homework.

208. Talk to parents about organizing the study environment and study supplies at home.

Parents are essential in providing encouragement and an environment conducive to study at home (see Strategy 54). Homework is best done at a location near the rest of the family, usually the place where the family computer is located. Kids don't feel isolated or exiled and parents can keep an eye on homework and computer usage. The area should be reasonably quiet, well lit, and the TV should not be on. However it should not be so quiet that it is not a stimulating environment.

209. Encourage parents to allow their underachievers to pursue out-of-school interests.

When a child does poorly in school, the first reaction most parents have is to withdraw a pleasant activity from the child as punishment. When this activity is the child's "passion area" this is the worst thing a parent could do. Studies have shown that underachievement is more likely to be reversed if underachievers are allowed to pursue an out-of-school interest that brings success. This success heightens self-esteem and leads to more success, and eventually may lead to a reversal of the underachievement.

Chapter 6

FLEXIBILITY AND CHANGE
WITHIN THE SCHOOL SYSTEM

> *I was presenting a workshop about underachievement to a group of highly knowledgeable and enthusiastic teachers. At lunch time we sat together and informally discussed the topic. "Our main problem with underachievers," these teachers said, "is not what goes on in our individual classrooms. It's the attitude of the administration and the inflexibility of the school system itself. We don't think much significant change can come for underachievers until the attitude of the leadership within our school district changes."*
>
> *The strategies offered in this section address some of the changes that need to occur at the district level. Some are strategies that can be implemented by individual teachers, but others must be addressed at the administrative level. These strategies, therefore, are particularly for school administrators as they search for solutions to the underachievement problem.*

Successful Strategies . . .

210. Apply for grants that facilitate and encourage change.

Grants are available from a variety of sources at the local, state and national level. Government agencies and private corporations provide funding to facilitate innovations at the classroom, school, or district level. Plan an innovative program aimed at helping underachievers and apply for grants to help fund it. Several of the other strategies listed below require additional funding. Grants are a resource to use in implementing these strategies.

211. Make sure district and school administrators are aware of the particular needs of underachievers.

All school administrators know that underachievers exist, but some are not aware of the needs of this specific student population or of strategies to use in meeting these needs. An in-service program for school administrators focusing on underachievement, its causes, and strategies for dealing with it would be very beneficial in planning programs to meet the needs of these students.

212. Provide release time for teacher training about underachievement.

Underachievers present problems and are the cause of much frustration for teachers. Many teachers have not had the opportunity to learn about underachievement and strategies to use with such students. This is a topic of high interest to teachers and one in which they desire more knowledge and training. Providing the time for attendance at in-service sessions about underachievement is a first step in helping teachers to help these students.

213. Have a small student/teacher ratio.

Many of the strategies discussed in this book that work with underachievers require personal, individualized attention. A small student/teacher ratio increases the opportunities for teachers to do individualized counseling, work to assess and remediate deficits, provide motivational activities based on student interests, and work with parents. Targeting specific teachers with special skills in these areas and finding ways for these teachers to have small classes will greatly increase the possibility that your underachievers will be helped.

214. Investigate ways to fund the purchase of enriching educational materials, supplies and equipment, including new technologies.

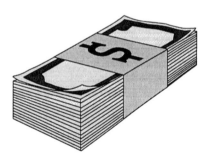

Enriching, motivational books, supplies and materials enhance achievement. Suggested titles can be found throughout this book and in the bibliography. The use of technology is also invaluable as a motivational learning tool (see Strategies 166-175). These materials and equipment require funding that is usually above and beyond the budgets of most schools. Investigate sources of funding, including grants and private contributions (see Strategy 210) that you can use for the purchase of these items.

215. Work to change attitudes at the district/state/national level regarding testing and the importance of test scores as the only criteria upon which to measure achievement.

The national emphasis on educational accountability has, in many cases, resulted in test-driven curriculum. Teachers teach a given number of instructional objectives at each grade level in each subject. There is little, if any, flexibility in what may be taught, thus no opportunity to work with individual needs or interests. The students are judged by their scores on a variety of state and/or national achievement tests. This emphasis on test scores and rigid curricular objectives makes it extremely difficult for the teacher to meet the individual needs of underachievers. These students do not respond like "average" students and are turned off to school because of the rigidity they find there. A greater emphasis on alternative assessment using student portfolios and projects based on student interests would be helpful to underachievers.

216. Provide for peer coaching and visitations to exemplary classrooms.

Teachers learn from other teachers. Every school district has exemplary teachers who have unique skills in individualizing instruction, assessing deficits, providing counseling, teaching study skills, etc. Identify these teachers and provide a way for other teachers to visit their classrooms.

For information on developing a Demonstration Classroom Program for your school district contact:

> Carolyn Coil
> Pieces of Learning
> 1990 Market Road
> Marion, IL 62959

or e-mail her at CarolynCoil@aol.com

217. Develop a well-articulated, district-wide study skills curriculum.

It would be helpful to underachievers if a curriculum to teach a variety of study skills were adopted by school districts and taught in the content areas. This curriculum would have a definite scope and sequence with skills that would build upon one another each year. Such a curriculum would start in the early grades and continue through high school.

218. Work with an organization such as a business partner, community agency, church, scout troop, etc. to create an after school program for underachievers.

Partnerships between school districts and outside organizations and agencies have increased in recent years. If such an agency exists in your area, work with it to develop a program aimed at meeting the needs of underachievers. Building self esteem, positive attitudes, skills in goal setting, organization, taking responsibility, learning styles, and the opportunity for hands-on computer experience are components of a typical program. Include parent training to increase their understanding of the characteristics and needs of underachievers.

219. Have teachers brainstorm their ideas and strategies for dealing with a specific problem with underachievers.

Underachievement is such an all-encompassing problem it seems overwhelming to many teachers. Taking just one aspect of underachievement at a time makes it a much more manageable problem. Use the form on the next two pages to structure teacher discussion and brainstorming.

220. Make all teachers aware of the factors that may reverse underachievement and use this awareness to develop a plan for working with underachievers.

Reversing underachievement is possible. Use the list on pages 107 and 108 as a discussion starter for teachers as they focus on ways to reverse underachievement in their students.

104

Characteristics and Causes of Underachievement

Below are a number of traits and problems that often cause underachievement. In a small group, choose one from the list, discuss it, and brainstorm strategies for dealing with your chosen trait or problem.

Behavior   ## Strategies

    Socially immature

    No goals or future orientation

    Behavior problems

    Lack motivation for schoolwork

    Negative peer pressure

    Low self esteem/self confidence

Family

    Family instability/problems

    Not firm; child can manipulate

    Education not a priority

    Too much pressure on child

    Not guiding child toward independence & responsibility

Society

    Little respect for teachers and education

    Culture glorifies instant wealth, glamour, sex, etc.

    School achievement not a cultural value

    Instant gratification the norm

Characteristics and Causes of Underachievement

Below are a number of traits and problems that often cause underachievement. In a small group, choose one from the list, discuss it, and brainstorm strategies for dealing with your chosen trait or problem.

School   Strategies

    Lack of variety in teaching styles

    Impossible standards or low expectations

    No patience with difficult/creative/divergent questions

    Overly helpful teachers

    Strict/repressive/inflexible teachers

    System inflexible in terms of meeting individual student needs

Student

    Fear of failure

    Academic holes

    No study skills

    Lack of organization

    Influenced by peers who are negative role models

Trait or Problem: _____

Best Strategies:

Reproducible pages 105/106 for teacher use.

Factors Which May Reverse Underachievement

Using this list as a discussion starter, explore ways you might help your underachievers reverse their underachievement.

The Student

* Area of high interest outside of school

* Self confidence/High self esteem/Overcoming fear of failure

* Developing strategies for independent learning

* Academic skills in "the basics"

* Ability to do long or short term goal setting

* Becoming organized and developing study skills

* Persistence and a willingness to try difficult tasks

* Positive influence of peers

* Development of leadership abilities

* Learning to deal with "the system"

The Family

* Positive parental attitude

* Support of out-of-school interests

* Recognition of a child's areas of strength

* Realistic, enforceable consequences for misbehavior

* Encouragement of responsibility and independence

The School

* A class of special interest in school

  - Challenging, differentiated curriculum

  - Independent study

  - Assessment beyond a grade on a test

  - Real life problem solving with ill-structured problems

* Classroom structure

  - Flexible

  - Creative activities

  - Allows for student choices

  - Considers learning styles, learning modalities, and multiple intelligences

* Use of technology

  - Independent research

  - Individualized instruction

  - Real world connections

* A significant teacher

  - Shows acceptance and caring

  - Communicates on a person to person level

  - Enthusiastic

  - Knowledgeable about content/subject area

Bibliography

Betts, George T. and Jolene Kercher, <u>Autonomous Learner Model: Optimizing Ability</u>, ALPS Publishing, Greeley, CO, 1999.

Canter, Lee and Marlene, <u>Parents on Your Side</u>, Lee Canter and Associates, Santa Monica, California, 1991.

"Cell Phone Homework Hotline," <u>USA Today</u>, April 24, 2000.

Coil, Carolyn, <u>Becoming an Achiever</u>, Pieces of Learning, Marion, IL, 1994.

Coil, Carolyn, <u>Encouraging Achievement</u>, Pieces of Learning, Marion, IL, 1999.

Coil, Carolyn, <u>Teaching Tools for the 21st Century</u>, Pieces of Learning, Marion, IL, 2000.

<u>Educational Leadership</u>, Vol. 57, No. 2, October, 1999.

Johnson, Nancy, <u>Active Questioning</u>, Pieces of Learning, Marion, IL, 1995.

Johnson, Nancy, <u>Questioning Makes the Difference</u>, Pieces of Learning, Marion, IL, 1990.

Johnson, Nancy, <u>Quick Question Workbook</u>, Pieces of Learning, Marion, IL, 1999.

Johnson, Nancy, <u>Thinking is the Key</u>, Pieces of Learning, Marion, IL, 1992.

Los Angeles County Office of Education, "Teacher Expectations and Student Achievement," <u>www.lacoe.edu/TESA/overview.html</u>

Minton, Lynn, <u>Parade Magazine</u>, May 9, 1991.

National Groundhog Job Shadow Day, www.jobshadow.org

Riegel, R. Hunt, Judith A. Mayle and Janet McCarthy-Henkel, <u>Beyond Maladies and Remedies</u>, RHR Consultation Services, Novi, MI, 1988.

San Diego State University, http://edweb.sdsu.edu/webquest

Schrock, Kathy, <u>Kathy Schrock's Guide for Educators</u>, http://discoveryschool.com/schrockguide/

Sisk, Dorothy, <u>Creative Teaching of the Gifted</u>, McGraw-Hill Book Company, New York, 1987.

Sprenger, Marilee, <u>Learning and Memory: The Brain in Action</u>, Association for Supervision and Curriculum Development, Alexandria, VA, 1999.

"Using Classroom-Based Performance Tasks," <u>Education Update</u>, Vol. 41, No. 8, December, 1999.

Whitmore, Joanne Rand, <u>Giftedness, Conflict, and Underachievement</u>, Allyn and Bacon, Boston, 1980.

Winebrenner, Susan, <u>Teaching Gifted Kids in the Regular Classroom - Revised, Expanded, Updated Edition</u>, Free Spirit Publishing, Minneapolis, MN, 2001.

Winebrenner, Susan, <u>Teaching Kids with Learning Difficulties in the Regular Classroom</u>, Free Spirit Publishing, Minneapolis, MN, 1996.

More Strategies I Have Discovered — That Work!

More Resources I Have Discovered